Psychic Gifts

in the

Modern World

Psychic Gifts

in the

Modern World

Gwin McGee

One Spirit Press
Portland, Oregon

© Copyright 2012 by Gwin McGee

All rights reserved.
Printed in the USA

ISBN 978-1-893075-99-3
LCCN: 2012934416

Cover Art and Design by Ethan Firpo
Book Design Spirit Press

This book may not be reproduced by electronic or any other means which exist now or may yet be developed, without permission of Spirit Press, except in the case of brief quotations embodied in critical articles and reviews.

One Spirit Press
onespiritpress.com
Portland, Oregon

CONTENTS

Dedication.....viii

Part One - 33 Years in Alaska...... 4

> The Gift • Growing Up in Alaska • Wedding In A Week • Starting a Family • Life Altering • Stage Two • The BEST Christmas Present • Paradise to Seattle • The Frozen North • The Rolfer • Solar House • True Alaskan Home • Wedding in Seattle • Back to Alaska • On the Road Again to Seattle • Next Stop Boulder • Back to the Frozen North •Opportunity Rocks • Rolfing in Hawaii • Home Ownership • Spirits Talk in Pictures • Manifesting a Dream • Man Out of Time • Advanced Rolfing Training • Home to Anchorage • California Dreaming in Seven Days •

CONTENTS

Part Two - Leaving Alaska to Live in Colorado...... 52

    Moving Away • The Visceral Training • Bio-Tec • Manifesting Steamboat • Healer or Scammer • Red Flag • Christmas at Vail • Patty • 2004 Graduation • Visualizing • A Small Plane • Gifted Chiropractor • 2005 Graduation • Friday Night Club • My Brothers Visit • Dragon Boy • My Friend • Drive to Seattle • Staying in Touch • Finding Help • The Shaman • Grand Canyon with Isaac • Turning Point

Part Three - Fighting the Dark Side...... 126

    Powerful Champion • My 54th Birthday • Reasons to Buy a Computer • Road Trip • Visit to the Psychic • Message from DL • Drive to Phoenix • Energy Vampires • Isaac's Gift • The Proposal • Visit to Mesa Verde • 55th Birthday in Seattle • The Wedding Dress • Lesson of the 3 Beings Lurking Energy Vampires • Skiing Winter 2011

Dedication

I would like to thank my Dad, Jim McGee, for helping me to be such a strong person. Thank you, Paul and Karen McGee, my brother and his wife, for supporting me after the death of my husband and for giving me so much support while training to become a Rolfer. Thank you, Paul, for letting me work on you even though I was a novice Rolfer.

Love, Gwin

Part One

33 Years in Alaska

Part One

The Gift

You would think it would be easy to have psychic gifts in this modern world. But to my amazement, it has often been a frightening and painfully awakening journey. You just can't drop into any book store and pick up a handbook that tells you how to deal with your unique psychic gifts (or at least you couldn't 50 years ago). If I had had the knowledge to tell my parents of my gifts, they would have definitely thought that something was wrong with me.

As a child, my parents were unaware that the reason I didn't start speaking until I was four years old was because I was communicating with them in my mind. Of course, being a child I believed that was how communication worked. But after a while I noticed that if I spoke words aloud, my parents promptly understood and answered me.

Do you remember when you were young, trying to imagine what you would be when you became an adult? Some of the picks were astronaut, doctor, nurse, or school teacher. I do not recall that professional psychic was on anyone's list of top career choices.

There was a time in the 7th grade when I was riding as a passenger in the car with a good friend and her mother. I remember seeing a red pickup truck coming down the road in our direction, and I knew at that moment that we were going to be in an accident. Then it happened. That red pickup truck ran right into us. But what was curious to me at the time was why no one else in the car knew of our impending accident?

Growing up in Alaska

My parents moved my brother and me to Alaska in 1967. I was 11 years old and was hoping that we would be living in igloos and traveling by dog sled. So, I was very disappointed upon my arrival in Anchorage, to find roads, cars, houses, shopping centers and many other structures of the modern urban American landscape found in the lower 48 states. Of course Alaska is also very different and more beautiful than the rest of the lower U.S., especially compared to Oklahoma and Bakersfield, CA, where I had lived with my family prior to our move north. But at the time, Alaska did not seem as exotic as I had imagined it would be.

However, once we moved to Alaska I noticed more clarity in my perception of future events that could affect my life. We moved from California to Alaska and as New Age sources report, Alaska existed in a highly spiritual energy grid. The population of Anchorage in 1967 was only about 40,000. So, I believe, the combination of higher energy grid and lower population per square mile increased my psychic clarity enabling me to perceive more information about my future self.

When you have psychic gifts, the first thing you need to learn is how to build filters in order to block out all the information that you are receiving 24/7. Luckily for me, I was able to build filters without even knowing what I was doing. During my years in middle school I began saying to myself, I don't want to hear those voices or know that information. That's how I started building my psychic TMI (too much information) filters.

The second hardest thing to learn when you have psychic gifts is to decide if your thoughts are your own or someone else's. This is much more subtle to detect. Even today, I still at times have trouble realizing that I am picking up on someone else's thoughts, thinking they are my own. One of the events that influenced my life the most was my marriage at the age of 18. I dreamed of my future husband's parent's house in Anchorage when I was in the 7th grade. The first time Gil took me home to meet his parents I was 15 and recognized his home as being the house in my dream. I didn't tell Gil about my dream because I didn't want it to be my last date with this young man. Even at this point in my life I had no clue that I had psychic gifts. I thought I was just like everyone else.

As a youth working to pay for my college expenses, I had the opportunity to work on the North Slope at the most northern terminus of the Alaska Pipe Line. Living and working on the North Slope sure beat my previous summer job at a fish cannery in Anchorage. After work, my mom used to make me take my clothes off before I came into the house because I smelled like stinky salmon. On the North Slope, I made beds and cleaned bathrooms in the BP (British Petroleum) camp, which was considered the Hilton of the North Slope work camps. It was hard work, but then at the end of the day I didn't smell like salmon.

During the time that I worked on the North Slope I had my first encounter with one of my guardian angels. Later in my forties, I met with a psychic in Boulder, CO, that could see angels. She informed me that I had two guardian angels that liked hanging out and watching over me. One of my jobs at the BP camp was to water the plants in the atrium. The atrium had an upper floor and a lower floor that could be observed through the dining hall. Standing on the upper floor of the atrium I was watering plants and almost fell down onto the lower level. As I started to fall I felt a hand pull me back. I turned around to thank whoever pulled me back from my fall, but no one was there. Strange? Looking back, it had to be one of my guardian angels that kept me from falling.

Wedding in a Week

Becoming good friends with the baker on the North Slope paid off big time for my wedding. Now, it is not very romantic being proposed to on the telephone, but I was only 18 and so excited about the prospect of getting married, that all I could say was "yes". The baker was pretty excited for me too, and offered to bake me a wedding cake. Not many brides can say a baker from the North Slope of Alaska baked a banana wedding cake for them and then had it delivered to Anchorage on a Lear Jet!

The week before getting the wedding cake, I asked the North Slope Manager if I could leave a few days early. Leaving the "slope" early is not an easy request to fulfill. Commuting to work entails traveling by jet 600 miles from Anchorage and then landing on a gravel runway near the Beaufort Sea in constantly changing weather conditions. So making personal travel requests, opposed to the regularly scheduled employee flights, is definitely out of the ordinary.

But luckily for me, the BP Lear Jet was making a run into Anchorage with just a few passengers on board and enough room for me to catch an early ride back into Anchorage. This was crucial, because I still had to plan my wedding with only a week before the big day. Getting to ride in a Lear Jet made me feel very prosperous and important. I took that as a good sign or omen for the impending wedding and my marriage.

Back to my marriage proposal. Being of the mindset that I was madly in love with Gil, it went without saying that when he asked me to marry him, I said "yes" with no reservation at all. We married young. Gil was 20 and I was 18, but it seemed to be the right thing to do at the time. The church my parents attended was an Alaskan log cabin church by the sea (Cook Inlet) and that was where we were married.

Everything for my wedding day just fell into place in the course of a week, a good sign that we were on the right path. The future would show that it was the right thing to do at that time. Another way my psychic gift has expressed itself in my life is the way I make decisions. I will make a choice sometimes and not be quite sure of the reason I made it, nor where the decision will lead me, but I still follow my inner voice without reservation. Then weeks or years down the road, I learn how that choice made in the past affects a certain outcome in the present. It was like someone was helping me make my decision that would work to my advantage even far down the line. Deepak Chopra calls this phenomenon "synchronicity", a concept I would learn more about in my late 40's.

Starting a Family

Even though Gil and I were married at a young age we both finished college before starting a family. I was 23 when I had my son, Isaac, at the Soldotna Hospital in rural Alaska. Staying at the hospital was great because the hospital had running water. My husband didn't have the plumbing working in the new house he was building for us by the time of Isaac's arrival. So I informed Gil that I was just going to stay in the hospital until our home had running water! We had just bought a washer and dryer. But the washer wasn't much help without water. So after my threat of not coming home, my husband got the plumbing project done faster than he had ever finished a home building project before!

Gil wanted his growing family home ASAP. He loved babies. When he would come home from work he didn't ask me how my day had gone but instead asked, "Where's Isaac?" I've never seen a baby as content as Isaac was to be with his father. They enjoyed watching TV together among other things, but it was always entertaining to see.

During this time, I didn't think much about my psychic gifts, as I was busy raising my son living in rural Alaska, and trying to keep the home fires burning. And by "home fires" that is exactly what I mean. We heated our home with a wood stove, which is hard work. I became very proficient at splitting wood, starting a fire and keeping it going. I also dreamed of the day when I would have a thermostat in our home and a furnace or boiler. I do remember when I wasn't keeping the home fires burning I had time to crochet a blue and yellow baby blanket for my son. It was like I knew that my baby was going to be a boy.

By the time Gil and I had our second child, Jesse, I had gotten the home of my dreams and it had a thermostat. Today, I still love watching a fire in a wood-burning stove, but I'm always sure to have a back-up type of heating system with a thermostat to go along with it. While I was pregnant with Jesse I had time to sew a pink baby blanket. During August that year when our family made our yearly trek to the Alaska State Fair in Palmer, I also bought Jesse a purple teddy bear. My son was born in about 4 hours start to finish without any catches or complications. So Gil and I decided that it shouldn't be a problem to have the second child at home. The Alaska Dividend Fund Check (which is a state trust set up for all Alaskan residents to receive a portion of the oil revenues annually) would cover the cost of my Homeopath and mid-wife, and it also covered the home birthing class we took together. We even had money left over for some baby clothes.

Gil's mother was invited to come and take pictures at her second grandchild's birth. I think she would have preferred a hospital, because she spent plenty of time asking the homeopath what his qualifications were during my labor. I was sure I would have a girl, if the color of the baby blanket I made was any indication of the sex. But my mother-in-law was asking me what I would do if the baby was a boy. She was sure to remind me that she herself had had 5 boys. I replied that I would just have to give it back (but I was only teasing about that part). The birth of my daughter took 5 hours start to finish at our own home with no complications. We named her Jesse and she was a beautiful baby girl much to the amazement and surprise of my mother-in-law.

I seem to have a sense or inner knowledge that materializes in my mind from time to time. I can perceive information about a subject that I would often have no prior knowledge of. At the time I didn't think that ability was unusual, but it certainly drove my husband up the wall. He would say, "You can't know that. There is no way you could know that." I don't know why I had an understanding of concepts that I hadn't studied before, but certain information had just been there all my life. It's not an all-knowing knowledge about everything. It's just a knowledge I needed at the time to make supportive choices. There have been times when I would choose not to listen to that inner wisdom and let's just say I would have made better choices if I had listened to it instead. If I had possessed an all-knowing knowledge I would be a better speller and also wouldn't struggle with my grammar.

Parenting is a tough job and although anyone can have children, the hard part is in understanding what to do with them once you have them. I was very supported by the inner wisdom in raising my children. It gave me confidence and I knew what had to be done to meet my children's needs. I guess it worked out, because my children have turned out to be wonderful, loving, and productive adults. My question to myself is, "When you become a parent does your genetic coding kick in, or is it learned behavior from being parented?" For me I would have to say I received information above and beyond what genetic coding or what my parents provided me with.

Life Altering

My epic life altering experience that would change my comfortable current existence came at me in two stages. The first stage of my life altering experience was supportive and would prepare me for the second stage.

About nine months after my daughter was born in my dream home in the largest city in Alaska (Anchorage, which was also the city I grew up in) my husband decided to move the family back to Soldotna, a rural fishing community. Much to my disenchantment, I agreed to move back and live out in the middle of nowhere Alaska where everyone knows everyone else's business and/or is romancing someone else's spouse.

Let's just say I made the best of what opportunities were left open to me at the time. I started making all our own bread using a mill to grind wheat berries into flour. I became an amazing cook, cooking everything from scratch (and using as many organic ingredients as I could get my hands on is not an easy accomplishment in a small town in the middle of nowhere)! When you talk organic in Alaska you are talking hunting and gathering: what you can grow in your garden, picking wild berries, and hunting and fishing for wild game. My husband loved to hunt and fish above all else. So I had organic halibut, salmon, crab, moose and caribou. Another way I kept busy was to lavish a lot of attention on my children. By the time my son entered kindergarten he knew all his ABC's, could write his name, and could count to 100. He could also tell me all his favorite bedtime stories.

One day, one of my good friends in Soldotna told me she was going to quit her job and asked me if I wanted to replace her. I jumped at the opportunity. The job was working for a husband and wife chiropractic team as a deep muscle therapist. The couple, Bill and Kay, would be willing to train me in the art of deep tissue massage. The job was only 2 days per week, but paid $25 an hour. Woo Hoo!!!! A break from being a house slave, plus there would be adults to talk to, and I would have spending money and time to enjoy my children even more!!

I had never done any type of bodywork before. But Kay, the chiropractor's wife, taught me the basics. I guess I had some sort of innate concept of tissue work and so I worked on the neck of my first client with a degree of confidence. Later, Bill (the chiropractor) came downstairs and told me that it was the first time he had ever gotten this particular patient's neck to adjust. With that accomplishment, I was hired on the spot.

After a few months, Kay thought I had a lot of raw talent. She encouraged me to read a book she had by Ida Rolf on "Rolfing" and asked me to consider attending the Rolf Institute in Boulder, Colorado. It was amazing that in this small Alaskan town I would find a chiropractor that would have Ida Rolf's book and even more, that she would encourage me to read it! I had never heard of Rolfing, but while reading the book, I instantly began to understand the concepts of Rolfing and knew that is what I wanted to become... a Rolfer.

When I first started my new job at the Chiropractor's office I had no clue what direction I wanted my life to move toward or what type of job/career I would like to work in. I had just wanted a few days off from being a housewife and some spending money of my own. It seems the higher powers had their own plans for my career. At that same time another synchronistic moment of my life just fell into place. This was the first stage of my life altering experience that would support me for my next stage.

My husband and I agreed that winter that whenever I was ready to become a Rolfer he would accompany me to Colorado for my training. Gil seemed very pleased that he would be coming with me to Colorado. Once I had the support from Gil to become a Rolfer, I put the wheels in motion to become more independent.

I had a job again and I wasn't just the house slave anymore. I opened a checking account of my own and at age 28 years, I bought my first car. I loved being a mother, I loved having a family and now I was able to take care of my personal needs too. It was important for me to learn to take care of my needs before I could take care of the needs of my family. I needed to keep that passion for life burning in my heart so I could be a better mother and a better wife. Being a parent is a demanding job. But as a mother the work I did was expected rather than appreciated and I resented that. However, I was appreciated at work and a little appreciation goes a long way to help you feel good about yourself and keep that spark of life burning.

Three months had passed since I first started my job at the West's Chiropractic Clinic. I started to feel like I had some balance in my life. My son and daughter were in day care two days a week and loved going to play with other children their own age in a fun learning environment. I got a break from my children and enjoyed being with them more when I was instead of being worn down by them. It's hard for me to believe that I went to work two days a week and my job was so much easier than staying home. I was able to get some rest and sanity from being a stay-at-home mom. For the first time in my life, I had my own car and didn't have to ask my husband for money when I wanted to buy something just for myself. I started enjoying who I was becoming, seeing a better future for my family and feeling more passionate about the direction my life was taking. While being a stay-at-home mom, it can be easy to lose your identity.

Stage Two

On April 20, 1984, my husband, his brother Mike, and Mike's best friend died while commercial fishing. Their small boat sank in the frigid waters of Cook Inlet. I was now a young widow with two small children.

I'm sure at this tragic stage in my life the higher powers were helping me so that I would be able to move past my husband's death. I'm grateful that Gil's parents planned the funeral because at the time, unbeknownst to me, I was in shock. It was a beautiful funeral with a large bonfire on the beach not far from where the men drowned. There was also an amazing amount of food. I guess that's why they call it a potluck so you have lots of comfort food.

Gil's father George played "Amazing Grace" on the bagpipes while walking along the beach. It was the saddest, most beautiful moment I have ever experienced. I'm sure there wasn't a dry eye on the beach. After that performance I could no longer hold back the tears. Our pastor said some lovely words at the beach site; he was a man of love and insight. I have no memory of those words spoken that day, just the beautiful, sad notes of the bagpipes playing over and over in my head. For the final dedication of the day I was taken up in a small plane over Cook Inlet to release three dozen red roses above the three young men's watery graves. This was the second stage of my life altering experience.

To this day, I can't imagine the pain and heartbreak that losing two sons on the same day would have caused Gil and Mike's grieving parents. I certainly put in my days of crying and for the first time in my life couldn't eat a thing. I think I lost 10 pounds during that process and I didn't have any weight to lose. My friends and family members were becoming concerned. After about 6 months I started to put the weight back on to the relief of everyone but me. I wasn't even able to tell our son, who was 5½ years old, that his father was dead. Instead I asked our pastor to talk to our son and explain his father's death. He did such a heart-warming job of telling Isaac of his father's passing that all I could do was sit there and cry.

I felt like I had been in a dark hole for about a year after Gil had died. I guess it just took me that long to begin to recover from the grief before I could even start to think about living again. While I grieved, I kept working and continued to be a good mother. I went back to college and took a year of Anatomy and Physiology and a year of Kinesiology (prerequisites for the Rolf Institute). I tried to keep as busy as possible to avoid feeling the pain. The pain does soften with time and becomes easier to live with, but if it hadn't been for my son and daughter to love and them to love me back, the healing process would have taken much longer. I thank the higher powers that I did survive the pain because I began to have great appreciation now for the life I had been given. I was happy to be alive and my children brought me so much joy. My children became my friends and playmates. Children really know how to enjoy life.

My father was the one true person who was there for me while I was grieving. He made choices for me that I just couldn't make for myself. I'm so grateful to my dad for helping me move forward in life when I had no idea what to do next.

The BEST Christmas Present

That first winter after I lost Gil, my dad gave me the best present ever. He bought plane tickets for the three of us to visit him during the Christmas holiday on Ambergris Caye, San Pedro, a small tropical island off the coast of Belize. It was a celebration of birthdays of sorts. I had just turned 29 that October, Isaac had just had his 6th birthday in November, and Jesse and my father had turned 2 and 57, respectively, that October.

My dad, while in his 50's, seemed to be having the time of his life. He was living in a small condo on the beach with his local girlfriend Franny, swimming every day and occasionally sailing his 18-foot boat to Cozumel when the weather permitted. In the summers, my father commercial fished and gill netted for red salmon up in Alaska's Cook Inlet. He kept his boat docked near the mouth of the Kasilof River. Then in the winter he lived in San Pedro, Belize on a beautiful white sandy beach. Back in the 80's San Pedro was still third world living. But you don't need much when you live on the beach. His condo had one room, plus a bathroom. The floors were concrete and you could see the studs on the inside walls. In the one big room there was a stove, a sink, a few chairs, and a table.

The beds were made up of wood 4x4 posts and plywood. Foam pads were substituted for mattresses, which we all slept on. The small condo was comfortable and very cozy. It was like camping on the beach, but our shelter was more substantial compared to having a tent on the sand. The village had a satellite dish and my dad had a small color TV to keep up with world events. The bathroom had a toilet and shower with only cold running water and the water was kind of salty. Dad and Franny also had a cooking stove and refrigerator in the condo. Franny was a great cook and made the best ceviche. We washed our cloths in a bucket or sink and hung them on the line to dry. Shorts and t-shirts were easy to wash in a bucket, but blue jeans were challenging. I just waited until I got stateside again before washing my jeans.

I could look out the window of Dad's condo and watch Isaac and Jesse playing on the beach. The top Christmas present from Grandpa was the classic plastic bucket and shovel; perfect tools for building in the sand on the beach. Belize has the second largest barrier reef in the world. That makes for a calm beach with no crashing waves. It's the safest type of beach for young children because the ocean is very shallow. I was lucky to keep enough sunscreen on the kids and they were happy to stay on the beach and play in the ocean all day long.

It wouldn't take long before I saw my 2-year old daughter running around on the beach naked. I soon discovered why she couldn't keep her swimsuit on. When Jesse sat in the shallow water and played, her suit would fill up with sand and she would become uncomfortable. The quickest solution for her discomfort was to take off her swimsuit. I cleaned the sand out of her suit fairly often during the day in order to keep her suit from washing out to sea. My son Isaac enjoyed building roads for his cars and trucks he had scored this special Christmas. Isaac had gotten a model of the space shuttle from his Grandpa and to go along with his sand roads, he also needed to build a space shuttle runway.

San Pedro was small and our family walked from my dad's condo to the village on streets made of sand. There we visited the shops, restaurants and bars and located across from the town was a large Catholic church. The village had strong Spanish influence with many Spanish residents still living there. In addition, there was a large black population, descendants from the time of the slave trade. Belize had been a colony of Great Britain so the currency was based on the British pound. Add in the Americans that had retired there or had built hotels for the tourist trade and you had a very friendly diverse group of locals.

With a strong Spanish influence, the shops would close in the afternoon for the traditional siesta. My father was a strong supporter of the afternoon nap during the hottest part of the day. While he was napping, I would walk into the village to buy frozen fruit bars for Isaac and Jesse. The bars were made from the local fruit that grew on the island: coconut, mango, papaya, banana and so on. My favorite frozen fruit bar was coconut.

Paradise to Seattle

Isaac, Jesse and I spent a month with my dad enjoying his tropical paradise and when the time came to leave I was not ready to return to the below zero weather of Alaska. On the way back to Alaska, I stopped to visit my brother Paul and his girlfriend Karen in Magnolia, WA, which is just northwest of Seattle.

It was great to see Paul. We had always been close growing up. He, too, had worked on the North Slope in Alaska, and then commercial fished and guided big game hunts. He moved to

Seattle just before my daughter Jesse was born in order to go to school and learn the refrigeration trade. I didn't get to see Paul as much as I would have liked given our current lack of geographic proximity. But we had planned a ski trip to Crystal Mountain for the weekend after my month in paradise with Dad. Paul rented a motor home, which is a great way to travel with kids, girlfriends and tons of ski gear.

Paul and I grew up skiing in Alaska at a ski area called *Alyeska* in the small town south of Anchorage called Girdwood. We started at *Alyeska* when I was 12 and Paul was 10 years old. The mountain is very steep with 3,000 feet of vertical drop. It's a tough mountain to learn to ski on since conditions are often cold and freezing with ice on the lower slopes and near darkness in the middle of the winter.

My brother was always a better skier than I was in high school. But he was unaware of the advanced early season ski lessons I had taken from an instructor in Girdwood that fall. I was excited to show my brother what I had learned; I wanted him to see that I had become an advanced skier. The conditions at Crystal were perfect and the slopes had several feet of fresh snow that season. We were skiing on the groomed trails when I decided that I just had to cut down through the trees and make a few turns through the moguls. No big deal. I had gotten in quite a few days skiing the early season and the bumps were easy for me. My brother followed me down through the moguls and much to my surprise he had some trouble, fell, and then like a yard sale his equipment was spread out all over the ski slope behind me. Boy, was Paul mad at me! He refused to ski with me the rest of the day. But Paul is a sweetheart and never stays mad for long, so I was very happy to see him in good humor for our drive home.

The Frozen North

Back home to the frozen north to finish out winter and the ski season. The month long holiday kept me from thinking of past holidays with Gil's family. Every time I would spend time with Gil's family it was just a reminder of what I had lost. Isaac and Jesse were happy to be home and enjoy hot baths once again. They liked the beach and warm weather of Belize but they hated those cold showers. When you're no longer in the tropics and it's cold outside in Alaska, there's nothing better than a hot shower or bath to warm you up.

I was still going to college and working, but the children and I would spend the weekends in Girdwood skiing. Isaac took ski lessons in the morning and Jesse was in day care. I would ski with friends in the morning and spend the afternoons skiing with my son.

Alyeska is a local mountain so I knew most of the skiers and families there. Often I would bump into some friends from high school and we would end up skiing together. It would be the same for my son. He would end up skiing with friends from his class at O'Malley Grade School. Skiing helped me take a break from all the pressures of my life. It provided quality time for me to spend with my children and allowed me to enjoy life again without Gil.

The Rolfer

It just so happened that a Rolfer was working in Soldotna for the summer after Gil's death. One of the requirements for the RI (Rolf Institute) is to receive a "10 Series of Rolfing." The "10 Series" is the nuts and bolts of Rolfing; it deals with balancing the fascial planes of the body. How amazing it is that the Universe was not going to neglect its plan for me to become a Rolfer. In the summer of 1985 I received my first Rolfing session. I had been asking myself for a while "What is Rolfing?" Rolfing is a hands-on technique that lengthens connective tissue (CT). An injury can shorten CT disrupting the alignment of the entire structure or body. Rolfing lengthens CT and restores alignment to the body, thereby improving movement and reducing pain.

It is a process of lengthening the connective tissue (CT) in your body. CT is called the organ of support. It is the ligaments, tendons, and fascial plane that create the shape of your body. CT holds you together and tells your brain where your body parts are and coordinates your ability to walk in the field of gravity. My next question was how does it help me if my body segments are aligned so I can move better in the field of gravity?

I need to back up a bit here to answer that question. I need to talk about a fall I had when I was 7 months pregnant with my son. Gil and I were working on the old house, the one we heated with the woodstove. That house didn't have a foundation. It was on pylons so you could see underneath it. Gil and our closest neighbor built a block basement so the house would have a foundation. Before we moved the house onto the top of the basement I was pulling nails out of the 2 x 6 sole plate and fell off the block wall onto my hip. After that fall I began to have sciatic nerve pain, pain that ran down the back of my right leg. As fate would have it, I went to the same chiropractor for adjustments after I fell off the foundation wall that I would eventually work for when we moved back to Soldotna!

After we moved back to Soldotna and I started working for Dr. West he started working with my SI problem again. The chiropractor treatments helped, but the pain did not completely go away. I remember thinking at the time if I have this much pain at 28 years what am I going to expect when I turn 40? After two sessions of Rolfing the nerve pain from my SI joint that ran down the back of my right leg was gone. The two Rolfing sessions had balanced my ilium (created balance in my pelvis) and took the pressure off my sacrum and sacral nerves. Now you know why being aligned in gravity is a good thing. It gets you out of pain. (FYI, when I turned 40 I was pain free!)

I still had eight more sessions of Rolfing to receive, but I couldn't imagine feeling any better. To my amazement, with each session my body felt freer, lighter, more energetic…and the freedom I experienced skiing after a "10 Series" of Rolfing, well, I was wondering whose super athletic body was I skiing in. Oh, that's what a Rolfed body feels like, like getting a new body that's supple, limber, high energy and pain free! I was so impressed with Rolfing and glad that the higher powers were keeping me on course to become a Rolfer.

Solar House

That summer of 1985 I sold the second Soldotna house Gil and I had purchased together. It was the home where we lived when Gil died. I sold all the furniture to my wonderful supportive neighbors. My neighbors knew I had recently been widowed and when people heard that I was selling everything they showed up and bought everything I put up for sell at a good price. How thoughtful of my neighbors to help me out like that. I owned two acres of land near the old house Gil and I had lived in, the house we heated with a wood stove. So I decided to design and build a passive solar house. My brother-in-law Tim was a builder and because he was such a sweetheart he helped me build my new dream home. The two acres of land located off Gas Well Road was on a hill with a wonderful 360-degree view. What a great location! On a clear day I could see Mount Denali from the upstairs bedroom.

However, I ran into a small hang-up with the bank... something about a woman "not being an acceptable contractor." That's why I sold the house I lived in, my new car, my son's new bike and all the contents of the second home in Soldotna to pay off what I owed the bank. Then I turned my new house over to a local builder to finish. I traded my unfinished house for two acres of land across the Kenai River. Because I had nothing to keep me busy and no place to live, I decided it would be a good time for me to get out of Alaska and skip winter. I charged three plane tickets on my Visa card, and with only $35 in my purse and my children in tow, we all caught a plane to Seattle to live with my brother and his girlfriend that winter.

True Alaskan Home

Before the three of us jumped on that plane for Seattle we stayed a short while with George and Judy, the children's grandparents. This was Gil's childhood home where he grew up with his four brothers. It was also the home I dreamed about when I was in the 7th grade! I had never shared this type of information with people, fearing they would think I was nuts, and so I never felt it proper to share this fact with Gil's parents.

The grandparents bought the house that overlooked Hidden Lake from the family that had homesteaded the area back in the 50's. I know that Gil's family home survived the 1964 earthquakes that took out half the city of Anchorage. The house sits in the middle of ten acres and has a two-acre lawn that I know the boys hated to mow during the summers. The homestead has a panoramic view of Cook Inlet, Mt. Denali, Hidden Lake and Flat Top Mountain.

Flat Top Mountain is part of the Chugach Mountain Range that begins behind George and Judy's home and extends 250 miles northeast and is around 60 miles wide. The Chugach Mountains are part of the Alaskan State Park and it is where George tended a trap line and bow hunted for moose with his five sons. Their home is very Alaskan, with beautiful furs of lynx, wolverine, fox pelts, and bear rugs hanging on the walls. And an assortment of mounted big game heads including caribou and a buffalo skull over the fireplace. I have always liked the buffalo skull.

So we are talking about a real time Alaskan family. It was always a treat for me to have dinner with Gil's family when we were dating in high school. One weekend when I was hanging out with Gil, he wanted to show me what his brother Tim had in his bedroom. I was more frightened than surprised to find a full-grown bald eagle there. An adult bald eagle has a huge wingspan. I remember it covering Tim's bedroom from wall to wall. He had a permit to keep injured birds until they could be released back into the wild. My question to Tim was how did he feed his eagle, to which he responded, "I let a live mouse loose in the bedroom, then close the door."

It was the night before our departure from Anchorage. Isaac and Jesse were sleeping in Tim's old bedroom and I was sleeping in Gil's old bedroom. Just before I drifted off to sleep I sensed a presence outside the window looking in, but I didn't see anyone. In Alaska in the summer it doesn't get dark outside so had a person been standing outside the window I would have seen them. Then I felt the energy of a presence enter the room. Shortly thereafter I heard my husband's voice start talking to me, telling me how sorry he was that he had left me to raise our two children alone and that he wished he had been more careful. He also said he wished he had appreciated his life and family more. Now that he was unable to be in the physical world he felt much regret and sorrow. He wanted me to know how much he loved me, and the children, and he wished he could be with us. At that moment I was scared. My answer back was for him to go away because he was frightening me. I quickly moved to Tim's room to sleep with my daughter in her bed. After a short while I felt my husband's presence leave.

It took a few days for me to compose myself and understand what had happened that night. During the time I was in high school I had felt that type of energy presence before. I worked very hard to ignore those energetic presences and when I did so, they would go away. It dawned on me that I was able to feel and hear my family members after they had died. Another aspect of my gift was emerging at the age of 29. I put this new information on the back burner and spent the winter in Seattle with my side of the family.

Wedding in Seattle

I was still grieving and I didn't want to think about my life before Gil's death. Seattle in 1985, before the boom, was a fun city, easy to get around in, and not much traffic. We lived in Magnolia just a few blocks away from my brother and his girlfriend.

That winter Paul and Karen were married. I was so happy to be there for my brother's wedding. Karen, my new sister-in-law, was a great friend and she loved helping me with Isaac and Jesse. I was very grateful for all her help during that period of my life when my need for support was great. Discovery Park was just across the street from where Paul and Karen. Two or three days a week, Karen and I would take Isaac and Jesse for walks in Discovery Park. The winter I spent in Magnolia, I got hooked on MTV and 80's music. At that time, MTV actually played music videos 24/7 which was quite entertaining.

I bought an S-10 Chevy Blazer 4X4 while I lived in Seattle that winter and for the first time in 10 years it snowed over a foot. Evidently, the higher powers were making sure that I picked the right type of vehicle for the snowy weather.

Back to Alaska

It also had been a good choice for me to spend the fall, winter, and spring in Seattle with my side of the family. My dad and his new wife (Franny, the girlfriend from Belize) stopped in Seattle for Easter before heading up to do some commercial fishing in Kasilof, Alaska. At the end of May, I drove back to Alaska with the kids in my new SUV to go to work for West Chiropractic again that summer. I made a bed in the back with a foam pad and I put all of our suitcases under the foam pad so it made a great place for the kids to play and sleep. I wanted to make the trip fun and comfortable for Jesse, now 3, and Isaac, 7. It's a long hard 4-day drive to Alaska from Seattle including hotel stops each night with 12-hour days, and over 2,410 miles of travel.

On our way to Alaska we stopped in Vancouver, BC for the '88 Expo. The band Lover Boy was playing in concert. We had the luck to be at the Expo the day Prince Charles and Lady Diana made an appearance in their top down motorcar. My son had ridden the roller coaster so many times that day that by the time evening rolled around he was one sick child.

I was very excited to be back in Anchorage, until I noticed all the snow still on the ground. This was slightly disconcerting after driving five days and leaving beautiful green Seattle. I had many friends in Soldotna and my plan was to house sit all summer for two different friends that were out of town so I wouldn't have to pay rent.

I was very grateful for the support that summer and to have two lovely homes to live in. The first home we stayed in was built on the Kenai River with a greenhouse located in the center of the home. The side of the house that faced the river was all glass. I spent many hours listening to *The Innocent Age* album by Dan Fogelberg and watching the river flow and moose drink at its banks.

I spent the summer in Soldotna to rest up and organize my life. I worked at the West Chiropractic Clinic for spending money. I also had to write a 40- page paper as a requirement for acceptance into the Rolf Institute. I'm not a writer. I'm a storyteller. So it took me the entire summer to write 40 pages about joint and muscle movement and what Rolfing is and how it affected me. Being an Alaskan resident has its privileges. I was able to take out a student loan from the state of Alaska in order to help pay for my Rolfing training. I needed to get all the paper work done and have the money to start school that October. Gil's parents were so gracious to help me pay for those expenses of schooling that the loan did not cover.

I finished my paper by the end of summer and was praying it would get me accepted into the Rolf Institute (RI). I received my paper back in September, saying I was accepted, just in time to drive back to Seattle. The remarks on my paper were passing; they liked my story of how Rolfing had changed my reflexes and how fast I could catch my toothbrush and keep it from falling into the toilet. But I was a little weak on my number of references. However, I had had two years of doing bodywork at the West Chiropractic Clinic and I knew I could handle being a Rolfer.... piece of cake.

On the road again to Seattle

Back on the road again and another 2,410 miles in order to return to Seattle. To this day, my kids don't care for long road trips. My brother and his wife were very supportive of me becoming a Rolfer. They made it easier for me to achieve my goal. I was so grateful for all the times Paul and Karen let my family live with them. It would be free Rolfing for life for my brother and his family. When I arrived back in Seattle in September, I lived with Paul, Karen and Karen's two yellow cats in Federal Way. The best part of living in Federal Way was walking down to the waterfront from their apartment.

A special day for me was when my brother would take me to the commercial district near the docks of Seattle to buy parts for his business. I thought my brother was so cool. He had one of the first cell phones that was attached to a large battery that was almost the size of a car battery. I'm sure it was like carrying around a bowling ball. Paul was working in Seattle at the time and wanted to be closer to downtown. Within the month we all moved to Freemont.

Paul had a fishing buddy from Alaska that owned a condo on Lake Union. We were within walking distance from Freemont and Gas Works Park. Karen and I would take Isaac and Jesse for walks in the park and Jesse would push her birthday doll in her stroller until she wore herself out; then Jesse would ride in her stroller with the doll. On cooler days we would bundle up Isaac and Jesse and walk to the docks to feed the ducks. In the morning, looking across Lake Union, I would watch the sunrise reflect multi-colored pinks across the glass of the high-rises in downtown Seattle. The view of Seattle across Lake Union was always stunning no matter the time of day. Living next to the shore of Lake Union was one of my most memorable residences during my stays in Seattle.

Next Sop Boulder

By the first of October it was time to drive to Boulder, CO to start Rolfing School. We only hit one blizzard, which was in Wyoming and I was so happy that I had bought an SUV (thank you higher powers). I stopped in Denver to visit Gil's best friend from college, Kevin. During our college days Kevin was easy to pick out in a crowd because of his long red hair. We first met at Western State College in Gunnison back in the 70's. Kevin, Gil and I all skied together for four years at Crested Butte while working on our Bachelor degrees.

I found a great furnished apartment in south Boulder for $600 a month. And I found a wonderful nanny for Isaac and Jesse. I love it when a plan comes together. However, I was a little shocked to see the Rolf Institute (RI) for the first time. It was an old fire station remodeled to be a school. I was expecting a grander building. But I realized, like most great things, that it's not the package, but the content inside. I was already in Boulder so I thought I might as well check out the school.

I still had one hurdle left before I was accepted into the RI. I signed up for the October auditing class, thinking how hard could the interview be to get into that first Rolfing class? The interview seemed to have quite a few people distressed; one person was in the bathroom hanging over the toilet sick. All I could think of was, are you serious? I enjoyed my interview. I thought all the teachers and those Rolfers that were taking part in the interview process were kind and had the intention of making sure all students were able and willing to make a commitment to the training process.

What I would find out years later from one of the teachers (Ray) who had asked me questions during my interview, was to everyone's amazement, how serious I was about the training. He told me later that they had no intention of turning me down. After all, my husband had drowned fishing two years before and I had driven down from Alaska to Boulder as a single mom with my two children. They seemed to think I had more than enough commitment and fortitude to make it through the Rolfing training.

Once auditing started and the teachers began teaching I knew I was in the right place. How does the saying go? I took to Rolfing like a horse takes to running. During auditing I observed and listened to all the lectures. I watched the students in the practitioner group Rolf models. I really excelled in class and understood the information presented, but some days it was hard to just watch and not participate. I'm a hands on person and the auditing phase of the RI sometimes made me feel drowsy while watching the models get their Rolfing sessions. I was ready to be a practitioner and start doing bodywork myself! But when I trained at the RI, there was a policy that students had to take a four-month break between the academic portion and the practitioner portion of Rolf training. The RI wanted the information their teachers packed into your brain to percolate. I found that policy to hold true, because over the course of that four-month break my understanding of Rolfing became much clearer. It was like putting a puzzle together... the more pieces of the puzzle I was able to put together, the clearer my vision of Rolfing.

While I was attending the RI, my daughter turned 4 years old. Her only wish that year was to celebrate her birthday at McDonald's. The McDonald's on Table Mesa Drive in Boulder had only a small outdoor slide and a few plastic animals to rock back and forth on, but she loved it anyway. It's a good thing we were in Colorado because in Alaska we all would have been freezing outside. I always love getting out of Anchorage in the winter. October in Boulder still has some warm sunny days. My son turned 8 that November. He was older and wanted his birthday party at home with birthday cake, ice cream and some of his friends from his new grade school in Boulder. Isaac and his friends had a warm sunny day in November, the best kind of day to enjoy playing outside and celebrating a birthday.

Despite the good weather that fall, I didn't want to spend my four month long break in snowy Colorado, so I packed our things into the S-10 and drove back to Seattle. We spent the rest of winter without snow and living with Paul and Karen on Lake Union. Gas Works Park was again a favorite of Isaac and Jesse, and we would walk there almost every day. Once a week we walked down to the docks with Karen to feed the ducks and watch the ducks swim around in the water chasing bits of bread.

Spring was approaching and so was the time for me to return to Boulder. My kids enjoyed the drive back this time because I let them eat at McDonald's and swim at the hot springs in Glenwood, Colorado. As a mother I loved spending time with my children and keeping my little campers happy.

Back in Boulder, this time my children and I lived in a much smaller one-room apartment with a swimming pool for this second and last phase of my Rolf training. The children loved to play in the water, so I couldn't refuse their request for a pool. Isaac and Jesse didn't care that we all slept in one room because they had their own swimming pool that they could spend all day in. And across the street was a huge park with swings. Kids are so happy, so easy to please at that young age.

Back for the second half and final phase of my Rolfing training I would be the practitioner while the auditors watched me Rolf the models. Yeah! During the practitioning phase, we picked partners in our group to exchange bodywork with. We each had to give and receive ten sessions of Rolfing. On top of getting ten life changing sessions of Rolfing, we also took our partner and two other models through 10 sessions of Rolfing. It was a very demanding eight weeks of training.

The lead teacher in my practitioner class was Stacy Mills. Stacy had trained with Ida Rolf and now 73 years old she was teaching my class. She was one of the most outstanding woman role models of my life. It assured me that there was productive life after the age of 40, and I was only 31 at the time. Stacy was a beautiful woman. She looked to be only in her 50's, her dress was impeccable, she spoke with intelligence and moved with elegance. Stacy had amazing insight into people and this led her students to find a better understanding of themselves. She was also a noted physiologist who at the age of 45 became a Rolfer. Stacy lived in Hawaii and held Rolfing trainings there in her home.

The assistant teacher was Ray McCall, a very talented Rolfer. I attribute my knowledge and strong foundation of the "Rolfing 10 Series" to Ray's teaching skills and body technique. He had a soft touch that changed structure without effort. During one day of class, I volunteered for a demonstration on how to create length in the rib cage and improve breathing. Ray only did one side of my rib cage and then we were dismissed for the weekend. Most days, including weekends, I would get up early for the sunny spring mornings and go for a walk. This time, I felt very lopsided while on my morning walk, like I was longer on one side than the other. Also, I could breathe much better on the side that Ray had worked on. My lopsided body was not happy, and I was so looking forward to Monday's class. Ray was very kind and worked the other side of my body, and balance was restored.

The whole process of learning Rolfing was nothing like my traditional education in high school or college. The selection process of the RI was such that only the students that had met all the prerequisites could begin training. Therefore, anatomy and physiology was already part of the student's background information. This inspired freedom in class to learn, grow and experiment. As students, we were all like a box of sponges trying to soak up every drop of information about Rolfing that we could. Our brains were absolutely full during the eight weeks of class. All we thought about was Rolfing in class and out of class.

There were no tests during the training but there were requests for notes, pictures about the sessions of each model that you worked with, about structure, rotation, imbalances, shifts that took place in the models, and what improvements and changes that had accrued during the Rolfing process. If your models changed (dropped into their feet, experienced lift in chest, could feel balance front to back, right to left and if the instructors could see these changes in your models) you passed. For every session the students and the instructors evaluated each model before and after the session. My model changed so much during his sessions that Ray would ask me what I was doing? I replied, Rolfing!

During one of the weekends that I spent with Jesse and Isaac, Isaac crashed on his skateboard and skinned one side of his face on the sidewalk. I was pretty sure that he would have scars on that side of his face for life. I broke open vitamin E capsules and kept his scabs covered with vitamin E during his healing process. Isaac was having headaches and the next day at the RI, Ray was working on kids for free. So I took Isaac with me to class. Ray McCall thought Isaac most likely had a mild concussion. Ray did some cranial work on

Isaac's head to help relieve his headache. Ray advised me that in most head injuries the cranial bones are pushed out of place and this causes the brain to swell. Ray shifted Isaac's cranial bones back into place and his headaches went away. I'm happy to say that the vitamin E healed Isaac's face with no scars.

At the end of eight weeks my two models looked great. The Rolfing student I trained with had received 10 sessions of Rolfing from me and had also regained the hearing in her right ear. One of my models was a bike messenger from Seattle. Needless to say he was hit more than once by a car. But by the end of his "10 Series" he was pain free and walking in a straight line. After my "10 Series" I no longer looked like I had spent the day out on horseback riding the range. Rolfing had taken the bowlegged-ness out of my pelvis and legs. I passed the class with flying colors and I was now an official Rolfer.

May 25, 1987, the day was at hand. Three years I had been planning for this day, the day that I would become a Rolfer. All that was left to do was pack up and drive back to Seattle. Before we could leave for Seattle I needed to make a stop at the record store for some cassette tapes and tunes for the long drive back. I liked Anita Baker's hit song "Sweet Love" and "So" by Peter Gabriel, as well as "Tango in the Night" by Fleetwood Mac. I purchased these albums and by the time we reached Seattle, Isaac knew all the words to the whole cassette tape of Fleetwood Mac. To this day I don't think Isaac or Jesse particularly like any of the music we listened to on our driving marathons.

Once again we arrived in Seattle for a short visit with Paul and Karen. I love Seattle because of all the green. I think while growing up in Alaska I became green deficient. Eight months of white stuff on the ground… I don't think that is healthy for me. However, I was looking forward to getting back to Alaska because I had many friends there, people I had worked with in the past, plus Anchorage had a healthy Rolfing population. It was going to be a good place to start my Rolfing practice. For the last drive back to Alaska I packed up again and in May drove the Alaska Highway North.

Back to the Frozen North

I was not sure at the time where I would be living for the summer in Alaska. Tim, my brother-in-law, wanted to know if I would be interested in living in the house that I had designed. The builder had finished the house and would trade back the land I owned for a down payment on the house. To my amazement I ended up living in the passive solar house I designed. My brother and father were commercial fishing that summer in Cook Inlet. Paul, Karen and Karen's two yellow cats lived with me in my Soldotna house over the summer. Dad and Franny lived in a friend's trailer and came by to visit (mostly to do laundry and take showers). But I loved having my entire family with me in my new home. I enjoyed having all the company that summer.

My Rolfing practice was very slow that summer and I had just a few clients. I didn't have much luck starting a Rolfing practice in Soldotna, which again is rural town by Alaskan standards. While Gil and I lived in Anchorage we would see a homeopathic practitioner for our health care. I spent a fair amount of time driving from my Soldotna home to Anchorage shopping for furniture to fill my dream home. The 150-mile drive to Anchorage, for me, was only a short trip. On one of my drives to Anchorage I stopped by to visit Wayne, my homeopathic practitioner. Wayne was planning to move his office to a holistic health clinic and wondered if I would be interested in working in Anchorage at this new clinic because the clinic was looking for a Rolfer. At this point, I began to think that my life was just one higher power intervention after another. I was grateful for the help and guidance.

Yes, I took that opening with the Holistic Clinic in Anchorage even though I lived 150 miles away. My plan was to work three days a week in Anchorage (Tuesday, Wednesday and Thursday) and then spend the rest of the time with Isaac and Jesse. I had some good friends in Anchorage who I could stay with two nights per week, and my old neighbors in Soldotna had three sweet responsible daughters who could watch my children three days a week while I worked in

Anchorage. I enjoyed working at the clinic with the other alternative health practitioners and had plenty of wonderful clients.

I liked working only three days a week, but I definitely missed being in my own home with my own children every night. After about one month of driving to Anchorage for employment the arrangement began to feel unsettling. So I decided it was time to move back to Anchorage because the clinic there had enough clients for me to work a full week full time. I would much rather live in Anchorage than Soldotna and wondered why I hadn't built a house in Anchorage. But I believe grief keeps you from thinking clearly. We moved to South Anchorage into an area called Independence Park, which was considered one of the best planned neighborhoods in Anchorage at the time. Independence Park had bike trails and sidewalks; such a great place to have my children grow up in. Isaac and Jesse could walk to the corner store and safely cross the street at the traffic light. The buildings were all new, the homes were affordable and I felt safe living there.

I found a nice new apartment in Independence Park and started unpacking. Isaac and Jesse felt like they had found paradise. They had bike trails, lots of new friends, and children their own age to play with. We were barely in our new apartment a week when Isaac and Jesse came home with exciting news: "Jeff and Jenny lived on the same street!"

Jeff and Jenny's mom, Barb, was a close friend of mine from Soldotna. Our sons were the same age and grew up playing with each other. Really, Jeff and Jenny lived on the same street? Immediately I walked down the block to visit Barb, and boy was she surprised to see me. We were both happy and comforted to be living almost next door to each other in Anchorage. What's the chance of that happening? Pretty slim I'm thinking. I knew for sure that Barb as my neighbor was a positive sign that I had made the right choice in moving out of Soldotna. I had never really liked living out in Soldotna and was so happy to be back in Anchorage. Anchorage, in my opinion, was the only place civilized enough for me to enjoy living in Alaska.

What to do with the house I designed in Soldotna? I rented that house to a family that liked living in Soldotna and enjoyed renting a new home for myself in Anchorage. Soldotna didn't have many nice homes to choose from. Most homes you bought you had to fix up. The Alaska dream, build your own home and live in it at the same time. What a nightmare. I never regretted moving away from Soldotna, but I DID regret not building my passive solar dream home in Anchorage.

I was happy to be living in Anchorage with a full-blown Rolfing practice. Isaac started the 3rd grade, Jesse started kindergarten, and both enjoyed their new schools and new friends. A big bonus of living in Anchorage was that we were only 30 minutes from *Alyeska*, the ski area where I learned to ski as a child. It is a world-class ski area with a breathtaking view of Cook Inlet from atop the high lifts. The mountains seemed to rise up from the ocean to meet the sky with 3000 feet of vertical drop and over 200 inches of annual snowfall. A five star restaurant called the Double Musky Inn is located in Girdwood (the town where *Alyeska* is located). It has amazing food and drinks, with the best margaritas in my opinion. There is nothing like the coconut batter salmon and a salty margarita after a day of skiing.

Life was good and the only problem I faced was too many clients to Rolf. I was getting tired, my body hurt and I started getting tendonitis in my right arm. I didn't have much energy left over for my life and at this rate I didn't think my body was going to hold up until my children's 18th birthday. The reason my body was having a meltdown was because I was Rolfing five clients a day, five days a week. This is too hard on a Rolfer. I should have only been doing ten or so clients per week. However, I had to cover my overhead at the clinic and so I wasn't sure what my next move should be.

Opportunity Rocks

When an opportunity came along for me to spend the summer in

Seattle at my dad's house while he commercial fished in Soldotna, I jumped on it. I knew I was being helped by the higher powers. I put all our belongings in storage, moved out of our apartment and drove my Grand Prix with Isaac and Jesse to Seattle. My children were not too happy about taking another road trip to Seattle. My dad lived in a lovely small home in Ballard close to Green Lake Park. Our summer in Seattle consisted of walking to Green Lake, sunbathing, swimming and catching up on rest so my body could heal.

My brother and Karen had bought a house in Ballard and lived near our dad. By this time, Karen had a yellow cat and a black one with a black masked face, white underside and white paws that Karen named Bandit. I loved Bandit; he was a smart cat with a charming personality. One evening when Isaac, Jesse and I went to visit Karen and help her feed her rabbit, we discovered that the rabbit had escaped its cage. The four of us then set off to hunt for it. Our plan was to herd the rabbit toward the backyard and then cage it. We found the rabbit, but even with two adults and two fast children, we learned that rabbits are hard to herd. Bandit liked to go for walks and followed along with the four of us. The cat noticed that the four of us were rather challenged with rabbit herding. When the rabbit would run under parked cars along the road Bandit would chase the rabbit out from under the car and then herd it toward the house. With Bandit's help, we were able to herd the rabbit into the backyard and then capture him. I was amazed that Bandit understood what we were doing and then helped us catch the rabbit.

It was nice to be living near my brother and Karen. They were always fun to hang out with. That year, my brother bought a Porsche 911. Of course, Paul couldn't wait to show me how fast his Porsche could go and for me, it was fun to see how well the car handled at high speeds. That summer Isaac, Jesse, and I spent plenty of time walking to save money on gas. It was a good thing that all we needed was within walking distance. Along with the walking, I also lost five pounds those two months because I couldn't afford to buy extra food. But there were some good deals too. For instance, when corn cost only a $1 for twelve ears, then we filled up on corn.

Our summer in Seattle was wonderful. I had a great tan and spent a lot of quality time with Isaac and Jesse just playing around. I didn't work all summer except when my brother needed me to Rolf him. It took two months for the tendonitis in my right arm to heal. After resting for that summer, my mind began to clear and I started thinking with clarity again. I needed to cut my overhead and Rolf fewer clients so I wouldn't damage my tendons and ligaments by over working. With this knowledge in place, I decided to work out of my home once I returned to Anchorage.

I was very sad when the summer came to an end, but I was happy to see Dad and Franny make it home from fishing. The time had come once again to drive back to Anchorage. This drive over the ALCAN (Alaska-Canada) Highway was getting old. I had made the trip ten different times and even for me, a person who likes road trips, ten times is more than enough. I vowed to only fly the next time I decided to leave or return to Alaska.

We did take the time to stop in White Horse, Yukon to soak at the hot springs. The hotel tourist rates had kicked in and I didn't want to pay $75 for one night in White Horse, so I drove over to the hot springs swimming pool to contemplate my options. While I was checking the rates for the hot springs I discovered the hot springs offered camping spots. Well, what do you know? We could rent a camping spot for $5 per night.

The three of us spent the night camping in the back of my S-10 Chevy Blazer. It's a good thing Isaac and Jesse were just small children because it was a tight squeeze for the three of us sleeping in the back of that Blazer. But we stayed roasty toasty warm all night long. The hot springs were housed in the same building with a home-style family restaurant so we had wonderful homemade hamburgers for dinner and learned from other restaurant patrons that the restaurant served a killer breakfast, too. So in the morning we soaked in the hot springs, took showers, and then had an awesome breakfast before hitting the road again. The simple pleasures of life... Priceless!

When we arrived back in Anchorage I found a nice town home for rent in Independence Park, with an extra room for my Rolfing practice. What a great idea, to work out of my home. I Rolfed a quarter of the clients I had before, but made about the same amount of money. While I worked at the Holistic Clinic in Anchorage I picked up quite a few clients from Soldotna. How amusing is that? While I lived in Soldotna I couldn't build a practice. But I moved to Anchorage and now clients drove from Soldotna to have me work on them! Once I started my home Rolfing practice, I would catch a small plane to Soldotna once a week and work on five clients, then fly back to Anchorage the same day.

My neighbor that lived across the street from me in Soldotna, John, was a dentist and a good friend of mine. He opened his own dental office and was the owner of the building. John had offices to rent and was so kind to rent me an office for just one day per week. On and off for about two years I would fly to Soldotna once a week in a small plane in all kinds of weather until I turned all my clients over to another Rolfer named Mark who moved to Soldotna.

Mark was one of my clients and was so impressed with the results he received from Rolfing that he became a Rolfer. Mark wanted to live in Soldotna after becoming a Rolfer and I was happy to give him all my clients. I was ready to give up flying to Soldotna once a week. I enjoyed flying in the summer, but during the winter, flying through storms could make the ride a harrowing experience.

Rolfing in Hawaii

One of the requirements of the RI was to take workshops in order to acquire enough credits to take the Advanced Rolfing Training three to five years after becoming a Rolfer. The first workshop that I took to earn credits was a four handed, week-long Rolfing workshop with Emmit Huttons on Kauai, Hawaii in February, 1990. February is a great time to be on a warm beach instead of up in the frozen North. Emmit Huttons was a person who embodied the metaphysical world. The Rolfing workshop was influenced by Emmit's metaphysical viewpoint. A four handed Rolf workshop means two Rolfers working together on one Rolfer. This type of Rolfing is energetic work with shifts or transformations in the body that are mind opening as well as structure changing. To do four handed work on a client you need to find the pattern of strain and shortening in the facial plans or layers that have misaligned the structure. The two Rolfers analyze the client's movements and alignment to discover the beginning and end of that facial strain in the structure. Rolfer A works on the beginning of the facial strain, while Rolfer B finds the other end of the facial strain. Once the Rolfers find both ends of the facial strain the Rolfers get their touch to connect through the facial layers. When the Rolfers find that energetic hook up with their touch in the facial strain (even very old facial strain and injury patterns) that strain can be released from the structure very quickly.

Mike was the Rolfer I partnered up with during this four handed workshop. Mike was a very spiritual, metaphysical Rolfer who possessed a great touch. He studied the energy of the *Kundalini* at an ashram. *Kundalini* is the creative life force of the Universe that exists in all matter and living beings. In the ashram he learned to tap into this limitless life force energy to find spiritual power and enlightenment. During the workshop Mike and another Rolfer worked on me during class. After three days of this type of intense Rolfing I had an amazing experience. I experienced what it is like to hook up to the life force of the *Kundalini*.

If you ever tap into the *Kundalini*, hold on to your head because what you thought was solid matter (like walls and rooms) stops feeling or looking solid anymore. I was very overwhelmed with the constant surges of energy throughout my body. Mark helped to calm me down by doing some cranial sacral work on my sacrum that calmed my nervous system down. Experiencing the *Kundalini* is like taking Mescaline or some other hallucinogenic drug. The American Indians would use Mescal or Peyote buttons for their vision quests and to help them tap into the life force of the *Kundalini* (named something else in Native American culture, but still the same life source). As I found out, you don't need drugs to get connected to the *Kundalini*.

The next day we talked to Emmit about what I had experienced. Emmit was excited to hear that I had tapped into the *Kundalini*. He shared with us that he could tap into the *Kundalini* and wander around for three days at a time enjoying the altered state of connectedness to the creative life force of the Universe.

This four handed workshop produced major changes in the alignment of my structure. By shifting the relationship of my legs to the first lumbar the Rolfing reduced my scoliosis by 55%. The workshop also exposed me to a new mind expanding sense of reality. It took about seven months to integrate all this work that I had in Hawaii. It took time for me to feel comfortable with that amount of structural change that accrued in my body from the four handed Rolfing. That much change feels like a merry-go-round going way too fast when all you want to do is get off and slow your life down. But once I became a Rolfer the changes to my life and structure didn't slow down. I just became used to the accelerated pace of change in my life. Also, I was blessed by being able to experience the energy of the *Kundalini* which changed my understanding of what it's like to be connected to the creative force of the Universe.

In the dawning of my psychic understanding, the question to myself was, why was I the only one in the four handed workshop that experienced the *Kundalini*? The realization illuminated my consciousness. I learned kinesthetically by picking up information from being touched by other body workers. That's why my clients looked so good at the RI. I would kinesthetically pick up the information by touch from my teachers and apply it to changing the models in class. I was a beginning Rolfer with years of understanding and I hadn't realized I was picking up the knowledge psychically.

Emmitt and Mark had studied for years mastering connecting with the *Kundalini* and I just happened to pick up the ability in three days. It was another case of me being a psychic and not distinguishing the thoughts of others from my own.

Home Ownership

In 1991 Gil's parents kindly offered to help me buy a house. I found a small three-bedroom home with an office in the same neighborhood of Independence Park. The house had a carport and a place to plug in my Ford Explorer during the winter. It was the perfect home for our family of three. Isaac and Jesse were so excited they had their own bedrooms. It was June 1991 by the time we moved into our new home and Isaac was in the 8th grade while Jesse was in the 4th. I was so happy to have my own home and office once again. We had a grand lifestyle and skied on the weekends at *Alyeska*. Isaac was in middle school and he took up snowboarding since that was a lot cooler than skiing. Then on Friday nights in the winter, it was family night. On Fridays we would buy a pizza from Little Caesar's and play board games.

In Alaska, because of the 20 hours of daylight during the summer months, you are lucky to get to bed before midnight each night. It's the time of year to make up for the long, cold, dark winter and get over winter's cabin fever. Alaskans enjoy as much daylight and warmth as possible before winter rolls around and takes away the sun and warmth with it. In the summer Jesse and I liked going to the Renaissance Fair. One summer Jesse performed at the Fair as a magical fairy and I made her costume. Luckily for Jesse, that June it didn't rain at the Fair and she looked pretty every night. Also in the summer I would take Jesse and some of her friends backpacking to tent camp in the Chugach State Park on the Power-Line Trail. The girls would try swimming in Hidden Lake. But mountain lakes in Alaska don't warm up too much in the summertime, so swimming was always a short dunk to get wet and then a quick jump into the sleeping bag to warm up.

My son spent all summer on his bike with friends. He would bike all over South Anchorage. Once Jesse and I biked up to Service High School with Isaac, but after 5 minutes we didn't see him. I was in good shape and rode my mountain bike many miles. It just amazed me to see how fast my son could ride without any effort.

His father had that same strength and endurance with no effort. Isaac was hard on bikes and that summer I bought Isaac a new GT mountain bike. It's a new bike! What could possibly happen to the bike? But one day he brought the bike home with a bent fork. Isaac had been riding his mountain bike down concrete stairs. I was surprised he hadn't bent the front tire or crashed. In his next mishap he broke the seat post off. Wow, how does my *Evel Knievel* son manage those feats of destruction on a new bike?

In August we just couldn't miss the Alaskan State Fair in Palmer. Isaac and Jesse loved the State Fair and so did I. And if you could catch a day at the Alaskan State Fair without rain, it is one beautiful sight to behold… tall snowcapped peaks surrounding the green Matanuska Valley of Palmer, 40-pound cabbages, plenty of rides for the kids, and beer batter dipped halibut. After the Fair we never missed blueberry picking down in Girdwood under the chairlifts. I like picking the big blueberries, because you don't have to pick as many berries to fill up a gallon milk jug. And of course the summer couldn't end for my children without Mom's famous blueberry pie.

Spirits Talk in Pictures

It was the beginning of fall and I was enjoying having my own home again. I was spending the day cleaning and catching up on household projects and for some reason I was watching TV that evening. It was unusual for me to be watching TV on a sunny day toward the end of the summer. It was my duty as an Alaskan to be outside storing up as much sunshine as possible before the dark winter days forced me indoors to hibernate.

I'm good at multi-tasking, completing home projects and catching glimpses of the news on the boob-tube (as I like to call the TV). The glimpse I caught was of a young girl from Glennallen, AK on her way home from school, now missing. Her picture was being shown on TV, but I didn't give the picture much thought. After all, Glennallen is a small town 200 miles from Anchorage on the way to Canada.

I was folding the day's laundry when my mind became hijacked. It was like someone showing me a home video. The young girl was showing me a picture of the pick-up truck she climbed into and the person who was driving the pick-up. All I could see of the abductor was someone black through and through. When I look inside a person to check out their energy and I see black, that means they are disconnected from the light, and are broken and living on their dark side. This is what the pick-up truck driver showed me, but I had no idea what this abductor's face looked like.

However, I did get to go along for a ride with the victim to see where her assailant was holding her captive. The detail was so clear it was again like watching a movie. The girl was fearful and filled with pain. I could feel all her fear and her pain. In my mind's eye I held her in my arms and gave her comfort the best I could. Since this was my first vision of a person asking for help, I had no clue of how to handle the situation. As I comforted the girl in my mind's eye the vision of her circumstance faded away. Then as I began to regain my conscious thoughts I found myself sitting on my bed with the laundry.

It took me a while to gather my senses before I recovered from the unexpected visit, and feeling the pain and fear of a young girl who was being assaulted by an adult male. I debated with myself for a while wondering if it would be appropriate to call the police. I was thinking there was a good chance that the police dispatcher might think I was a nut case. If my call somehow could help the young girl, then I had to give it my best shot. I gathered up my courage and called police dispatch. I reached a female dispatch officer and explained to her that this was my first call to the police I had ever made and it was to report a vision I had about the missing girl. I told the young girl's story, trying to recall every detail she had shown me.

When I finished my story I was met with an unexpected reply from the dispatch officer. She asked me if the girl was still alive? I was sorry to say that I had no idea whether she was still alive or not. The officer thanked me for my call. I was thrilled that I wasn't perceived as a nut case and I hoped that the information would help save the girl's life.

A year later, I received a call from the District Attorney in Palmer, AK. She informed me that several other people had called in to help with the case, but that my vision had been the most accurate given. She told me they were looking for something, but not to tell her what it was. As soon as she asked me the question I knew what they were looking for and I told them where it was buried in relationship to the building where the young girl had been abducted. She thanked me for my answer and that was the end of the call.

How did I know in that moment the answer to her question when I hadn't had that information before the call? The only other person that I have ever communicated with in the same manner as the young girl was my husband. My husband was dead but had not yet "crossed over" to the other side as I like to say and I understand that I have the ability to communicate with spirits that have not yet crossed over. My guess would be that the young girl in spirit form was telling me the answer to the DA's question to help catch her killer. The odds were good that when the young girl came to me in a vision she had already crossed over.

Afterwards, I thought that I might help solve crimes for a living. But upon some reflection, I decided that I would rather use my gifts for the living and build my skills as a Rolfer. It was uncomfortable and unfathomable for my personality to wallow in the dark side of humanity. I would rather work in the light by introducing people to the healing arts of bodywork. I would stay on the Rolfing course and find a way to complete my Advanced Rolfing Training.

Manifesting a Dream

My big dream was to take Isaac and Jesse to Disneyland. Before my brother and I moved to Alaska we lived in Los Alamitos, California.

We lived only 20 miles from Disneyland and we had no clue how close we were. We were only in grade school and the cell phone didn't exist in the 60's. I have fond memories of our parents taking us to Disneyland. My dad drove around for hours before taking us to Disneyland so we wouldn't know we lived only twenty miles away. When we finally made it to Disneyland the parking lot was surrounded by orange groves and it seemed we were far way in the country side. My favorite attraction at Disneyland was Swiss Family Robinson's tree house, then Cinderella's Castle, the tea cup ride and the Matterhorn rollercoaster, which I kept my eyes closed for the entire ride, only catching a glimpse here and there.

Being a single parent can be frustrating at times. Being a one income parent trying to give my children the lifestyle of a double income parents usually left me short of money. So I was wondering how I could afford to take my children to Disneyland. I knew that somehow it would happen. I would just put my wish out there and let the universe work its magic.

Man Out of Time

In November 1992, I met Tim, a beautiful man with a glowing presence. He first became my ski buddy and friend, and he lived in Girdwood, Alaska, near the ski resort *Alyeska*. We could ski to his condo from the bottom of the mountain. What I appreciated most about Tim was his love for children and that he was fun to be with. My son and daughter liked Tim right away and became very fond of him. Tim was a special person and I always thought of him as a gentleman and a true Renaissance man, a man out of time with the modern world.

Tim was a master carpenter who could build a house from start to finish or create a fine piece of furniture. I considered Tim more of an artist than a run of the mill nail-banger. I asked Tim to build a Rolfing bench out of pine for me so I could easily move it around my Rolfing table. Tim took one look at my old Rolfing bench and in two days came back with a finished bench. To this day, any other Rolfer that sees my bench has bench envy. It's not just a bench; it's a work of art.

Tim was also a master falconer and the proud owner of two gyrfalcons, one white and one black. He had raised these birds to hunt duck with and I always imagined Tim sitting on horseback holding his falcon, claws clinched on his gloved wrist, pursuing the sport of kings and noblemen. Even without a horse, Tim looked noble with his white falcon sitting on his gloved wrist.

I was once invited to go on a hunt with Tim, accompanying his black falcon and bird dog. It is amazing to watch the partnership between a falcon and dog working together to support the goals of a hunt. The day I was along the black falcon was hunting Canadian Geese. Canadian Geese are huge birds and falcons don't usually hunt them. But Tim's black falcon "Christy" wanted to please her master and if Tim wanted a goose then Christy would bring down a goose.

At the start of the hunt the falcon is released and the bird dog chases the geese into flight so the falcon can take its prey in the air. The geese fear falcons more than they fear man or dog. The geese were in no hurry to take flight even when the bird dog was nipping at their tails. Tim joined in to help the bird dog with its task. I couldn't believe my eyes… Tim grabbed one of the geese by its neck and the goose was still reluctant to leave the ground. Once the geese were unable to see the black falcon flying above them, half of the flock took flight.

The next part of the hunt is the hardest, keeping track of the falcon and being able to retrieve both the prize and one's falcon. Tim and his trusted bird dog followed in hot pursuit keeping track of where Christy might bring the goose to the ground. You are never quite sure where that might be. But on this hunt the prize ended up in someone's backyard. Tim is great at knocking on stranger's doors and asking for permission to retrieve his falcon and its captured prize. People are pretty friendly in Anchorage, more than happy to help and if their camera is handy will also get a photo taken with a falcon in their backyard. How many people can say they have had a gyrfalcon in their backyard? It is a majestic sight to behold.

I'm sure you have read of birds getting caught in the engines of jets and that is not a good thing. Tim was one of the falconers that hunted ducks and birds at the Anchorage International Airport in order to keep them away from the runways and clear of jet engines.

Advanced Rolfing Training

Three to five years after completing basic Rolfing Training, the RI requires every student to take the Advanced Rolfing Training. By the time the summer of 2003 rolled around I was looking at my very own personal seven-year plan before completing my Advanced Rolfing Training. Thanks to the State of Alaska, which offered school loans for Rolfing Training, I would actually be able to meet the RI requirements and become an Advanced Rolfer.

Once again Paul and Karen were there to support me. Paul and Karen had just bought "the farm" (the name I gave my brother's new home), 20 acres of land with an old farmhouse ready to be fixed up. Isaac, Jesse and I flew to Seattle to meet up with my dad, Franny, Paul and Karen for dinner. The plan was for Isaac and Jesse to spend the summer with Paul and Karen. Isaac, now 14, would be helping Paul re-model the farmhouse and Jesse, now 10, would be helping Karen by taking care of her cousins, Nicole, 2, and 6 month old baby Megan.

I helped Isaac and Jesse settle into their new home for the summer. It was hard to leave my children in Port Orchard because I knew I would miss them. With hugs and teary eyes we expressed our good-byes and I caught a plane to Denver. (Notice here I'm not driving again. Thank God.)

Unknown to me, the old Advanced Rolfing Training had taken a major transformation. It would be the newly revamped, first time taught Advanced Training. The students in the class would be like guinea pigs. I was happy to hear there would be a new advanced 5 series. Because in the old advanced 5 series I had to sit on the Rolfing table with my legs in a Z position, which was very uncomfortable. The work done on my legs while sitting in the Z position just drove torsion into my lumbar spine.

The new Advanced Training would focus on spinal mechanics and use joint mechanics to create neutrality in the joints. The major principles of the class would be "holism and integration". Since this was a pilot class I was very honored to be taught by two extremely talented teachers, Michael Salveson and Jeffrey Maitland. The class also had its share of talented students. Although challenging, I understood the new concepts of spinal and joint mechanics which renewed my sense of enthusiasm for the transformational quality of Rolfing work.

I became acquainted with Liz Gaggini while exchanging the joint mechanics we were learning in class. Liz is brilliant and she quickly understood the new concepts of the advanced Rolfing work. Liz eventually became a long-term friend of mine. Not only did Liz have a sharp mind, she also possessed a quick wit. Some days she would have the entire class caught up in laughter, including our instructors.

The Advanced Training took my Rolfing skill level into a third paradigm of excellence. If I had tried to finish my advanced class in the required 5 years I would have missed out on the best Rolfing class I had ever taken. I would never have mastered spinal mechanics or become so proficient at returning all the joints in the body back to neutral. It was amazing Divine timing in action!

I was sad to see my training class end. The teachers and students were exceptional, but I missed my children so much and couldn't wait to have them back in my life. I was also excited to use my new skills on my clients back in Alaska. Our class had a small graduation ceremony and party and then it became official: I was now an Advanced Rolfer!

I flew back to Seattle to be with my family. The farmhouse was looking more like a regular home with new carpet, paint, and a remodeled kitchen. Isaac and Jesse were so glad to see me and they were more than ready to return to their home and friends. They gave me the tour of the farmhouse and Isaac showed me all the work he had helped Uncle Paul with. They took me on a walk and showed me the small country store, which was 2 miles from the farmhouse and the only place they could walk to. My son had the record for the most shots of espresso consumed in a single visit: 22 shots! I asked Isaac how he felt after drinking that much espresso and he replied, "Not so well, and very dizzy."

My niece Nicole was having pain in her knee, so I had the opportunity to try out my new set of Rolfing skills and see if I could help her. I had Nicole walk for me and noticed that her right SI joint was fixated. Once I opened the left SI joint and returned the joint mobility back to neutral the pain was gone in her right knee. The new skill level I had gained at my Advanced Training course was working great!

I thanked Paul and Karen for taking such good care of my children and then my brother dropped us off at the Seattle Airport for the four-hour flight back to Anchorage. The flight was a good choice because Isaac and Jesse would have rather walked home than be stuck in an SUV for another four-day road trip to Alaska.

Home to Anchorage

It was the end of summer 1993, and comforting to be settled back into our own cozy little home. Once again, time for the Alaska State Fair, blueberry picking and shopping for new school clothes. In Alaska the summers are short and the fall even shorter. I'm always a tad depressed when the fireweed has only a few blooms left at the top of its flower signaling the end of summer. September swiftly follows summer and as the days became shorter long shadows of trees cast themselves across every road. The lakes will soon be frozen, and the cold winter snow and long dark days are only weeks away.

But this year I was looking forward to the winter. Isaac, Jesse and I had a great place to stay within walking distance of *Alyeska*. I loved Girdwood and skiing was the only way I survived the long Alaskan winters. Tim had great neighbors with a hot tub and a wood burning sauna. These winter toys are essential for the well-being of stiff and sore muscles after skiing all day on the steep slopes of *Alyeska*.

Anchorage to Girdwood is only a short 30-minute drive with no Winnebago or summer tourist traffic. *Alyeska* is a local mountain and never too crowded because Anchorage is a city of only 300,000 people. It's best when you have a place to stay for the weekend in Girdwood and can ski two uninterrupted days and take a soak in the hot tub after skiing instead of driving back to Anchorage. For me it was always an attitude adjustment that improved my outlook on life for the rest of the week.

Once in a while when I stayed at Tim's place in Girdwood, he would bring his white gyrfalcon into the condo for a late evening bath. Tim placed the gyrfalcon on her perch and set a tub of warm water on the floor. Tim and I silently waited on the couch across the room. Once the gyrfalcon felt the room was calm she would jump down off her perch, slowly move toward the tub and tentatively jump into the warm water. When she felt comfortable her excitement began to show. She would splash water out of the tub, dunk her whole body under the water, and you could see that she was thoroughly enjoying her warm bath. When she was finished with the bath, Tim would set her on her perch for the night so she could dry off. Otherwise, if Tim were to put her outside before her feathers dried she would freeze to death during the cold Alaskan night.

This particular winter flew by for me with one weekend after another of great skiing and wonderful evenings of warming up in the hot tub. Isaac was learning to snowboard and fell plenty of times beating up his body in the process. I spent many Rolfing sessions putting him back together until he learned the art of snowboarding. It was worth the work on my son's part, because he's now a graceful snowboarder who carves all his turns and can do so on both edges. Jesse and her best friend Sara tried out for the Spyder Racing ski program, although they were more interested in having fun than in becoming ski racers. Once the ski days were becoming sunny and longer we knew Easter was approaching, a holiday I always enjoyed.

That Easter, Tim taught Jesse and me how to punch small holes in both ends of our eggs and blow the white and yoke out of the shell. We were excited to learn the process was so easy. All the time we spent decorating eggs could now be enjoyed year round. The demise of the beautifully decorated eggs wouldn't have to come to an end after the Easter egg hunt. Spring would not be spring in Alaska without the Easter egg hunt in four feet of snow that still needed to melt before I would be able to see my lawn.

California Dreaming in Seven Days

I had been talking to Tim about my dream to take Isaac and Jesse to Disneyland during the winter. That spring when I hadn't even been thinking about Disneyland Tim brought up the subject once again. "I have brothers and sisters that live in California. I haven't been back for a visit in years. We could stay with my family to cut the cost of staying in California." I was so overwhelmed with joy and appreciation at Tim's suggestion and generosity. The plan was to stay in California for a week, visit Tim's family, and try to see all the sights we could squeeze into a week's trip. Tim is the youngest of eleven brothers and sisters, so there certainly wasn't a shortage of family to stay with while we were in California.

On the first leg of our trip we flew into San Diego in order to stay with Tim's sister Sue. On the first day of our vacation we drove out to the sand dunes with Sue's husband and spent the day 3-wheeling. Lucky for us we survived. Three-wheelers were deemed unsafe and have since been replaced with 4-wheelers. Growing up in Alaska I spent plenty of time riding snowmobiles. It was easy to show my son how to high mark on the side of a tall sand dune with the 3-wheeler. My son, Mr. Evel Knievel, was impressed by my skills and asked me when I had learned to handle a 3-wheeler? I told him I learned how to high mark with snowmobiles in high school and I just applied my snowmobile riding skills to this machine. That day even my son couldn't beat the high mark I had set with the 3-wheeler.

On our second day, Tim drove Jesse, Isaac and me to Sea World. Tim made sure we all sat in the top row of seats because those spectators sitting on the bottom front row all got drenched with gallons of water by the acrobatic killer whales. We thanked Tim for strategically seating us in the upper rows while we shared a laugh wearing our dry clothing. After Sea World we rented rollerblades and toured the boardwalk along San Diego's Mission Beach. It was April in San Diego and we were all in shorts and t-shirts enjoying the warm sun while rollerblading next to the ocean. Meanwhile, back home in Anchorage it was snowing and the temperature was below zero. Springtime in Alaska is often a good time not to be in Alaska. In contrast, eating fresh strawberries always makes me think of California and how nice the weather is there in the spring.

On the third day Tim's sister Sue and her daughter took us to the San Diego Zoo. As far as zoos are concerned I found the San Diego Zoo to be one of the most beautifully landscaped zoos I have ever visited. The day was low stress and slow paced as we enjoyed the greenery, calm walking and animal viewing. The San Diego Zoo was huge and we walked for miles before we lost the light for picture taking. By the end of the day my feet were letting me know I had walked a major amount of miles, more than I was used to walking.

On the fourth day we drove north of L.A. to stay with Tim's other sister. Their house had sustained minor damage in the Northridge earthquake that hit January 17, 1994. By the time we arrived in March, their home looked fully repaired. We spent the day visiting with Tim's sister and husband, telling us all the damage that had accrued to their house and how scary it was to have your house feel like it's going to fall down with you in it. Call me selfish, but I was relieved to hear that Disneyland was still standing.

On the fifth day our plan was to get an early start and miss the freeway traffic on the way to Disneyland. It was only 35 miles to Disneyland from Tim's sister's house so it should have been a quick 30 minutes without traffic. But we failed to start early enough so with LA traffic it took more than an hour. However, we did arrive and managed to park just in time to watch Disneyland open its gates. It had been 29 years since my parents had taken my brother and me to Disneyland. I'm not sure if it was to my surprise or horror to see Disneyland no longer surrounded by orange groves. Instead pavement, roads, parking lots and many affordable motels and hotels surrounded the famous park.

My big splurge for the trip was to pay for one night at the Disneyland Hotel. The coolest reason for staying at the Disney Hotel was being able to take the monorail into Disneyland. We dropped our bags off at the Disneyland Hotel and had breakfast before Isaac and Jesse's friends arrived. I had planned a treat for Isaac and Jesse. Peter was 14, Isaac's age, and Annie was 11, Jesse's age. They were the best of friends and spent time playing at each other's family homes for quite a few years. Peter and Annie had moved from Alaska the year before and now lived in Pasadena. In fact Jesse and Annie had been in Brownies together during the third grade. I knew it would be great fun for Isaac and Jesse to be with their friends so they could all ride the rollercoaster together. My plan was to stay away from the rollercoaster rides and spend more time walking. I was more than thrilled just to ride the Monorail. Tim did talk me into going on the log ride. The ride was fun until the end, when it fell off the top of a waterfall. Besides the scary free fall, I got covered with water as my free-falling log splashed into a lagoon at the end of the ride. My land legs weren't too stable after that one.

Tim and I were wondering why Disneyland wasn't very crowded and noticed there were shorter lines for the popular rides. We then came to the conclusion that people were reluctant to plan a Disney vacation after a major earthquake. Isaac and Jesse only had two days to explore Disneyland and their only thoughts were living the Disney dream. They made sure they experienced all the rides they had been dreaming of riding for years. And they experienced as many as they could with their friends from Alaska, Peter and Annie. When Peter and Annie's parents came to pick them up that evening at the hotel they were exhausted but exhilarated to have spent the day at Disneyland with their Alaskan friends. It was a sad parting for Isaac and Jesse and it would be the last time they would spend any significant time with their close friends.

I had no idea that Disneyland stayed open after dark. We went on this amazing night ride featuring a river through a European village with lit cottages and fireflies casting about. I had seen the ride as a young girl during the day, but had not thought much of it; however at night it was luminous. I felt like I was sailing by a true European village. Spending the late evening at Disneyland was magical for me.

When you spend the night at the Disneyland Hotel the fun doesn't end. That evening we dined at the Disney restaurant and while we were there Disney characters dropped by to visit with Isaac and Jesse inquiring if they were enjoying their stay at the Magic Kingdom. I distinctly remember taking pictures of Isaac and Jesse with Snow White at the dining table. After dinner everyone played video games late into the night. It had been a long day for me and I was ready for sleep. I decided everyone should turn in so we all could get an early start; only one day left in the Magic Kingdom.

On the sixth day breakfast at the hotel was relaxing. No driving in traffic to find a place to dine, no parking issues, no stress. Our second day at Disneyland started at the haunted house. After that we found the pirate ship flying the Jolly Roger flag. We gained safe passage onto the pirate ship and were glad that we weren't the people having to walk the plank. It was a great day of touring and being entertained. I didn't hear any protests from Isaac and Jesse about riding rollercoasters. They seemed content spending the day with Tim and me exploring the rest of the attractions.

That evening we stayed at an inexpensive hotel. I was ready for a quiet dining experience without the Disney characters. I'm sure by day six of our vacation I was reaching the point of sensory overload. By the evening of the sixth day, the week was becoming a blur of events strung together producing the best vacation that my children were old enough to remember and enjoy. My last night in California was a blank. I didn't even remember the evening or when I finally fell asleep.

On the seventh day, God supposedly rested, but we were up at the crack of dawn to see as many sites as possible on our last day in California. We were so early arriving at Universal Studios that we were the first in line waiting for the park to open. After purchasing tickets we started our day with the Back Draft attraction, which is a great way to reverse the chill of the morning air from waiting in line. I was certainly warmed up after that attraction and the Back Draft movie set gave us all new meaning to the phrase, "never play with matches." Isaac and Jesse's pick of the day was the Back to the Future ride. I was very impressed by the technology used to bring to life the fantasy of flying in a car. Then there was the ET ride which I called "experiencing the celestial life force on a bike".

Jesse later spotted Kitt the talking Trans Am from *Knight Rider*. It was a TV show that Jesse and I watched at home every week. Jesse had a long list of questions to ask Kitt and she was having way too much fun getting Kitt to provide explanations. Kitt finally asked my daughter to move along. We finished off our day at Universal Studios by dancing in the street to the Blues Brothers rendition of "Soul Man".

That afternoon we joined up with Tim's brother Joe who was such a sweetheart and also a talented sketch artist. A vacation to California wouldn't be complete without visiting Hollywood and taking the famed Walk of the Stars to view the numerous imbedded icons in the sidewalk. We searched for our favorite actors and actresses and then couldn't pass up visiting Grauman's

Chinese Theatre, built in 1927, where we took a family photo as evidence that we were all there.

    I would like to give thanks to Tim and his family for turning the dream I had of taking my children to Disneyland into a reality. We played for a whole week in California on a single Mom's income. I give thanks to the higher powers for helping me manifest a dream vacation for my son and daughter.

Part Two

Leaving Alaska to Live in Colorado

Part Two   Leaving Alaska to Live in Colorado

Moving Away

My deadline was approaching. My son was a wonderful help for me. At the time he was driving a delivery truck for Carlisle Trucking in Anchorage. Jesse's best friend Sara's dad owned Carlisle Trucking. So Isaac had access to the delivery truck. Once I had all my boxes packed and ready to go Isaac came over with his delivery truck and packing material. I had enough boxes to fill two pallets. After Isaac had all my boxes stacked nice and neat on the 2 pallets he took out this huge roll of plastic wrap and went round and round the boxes on the pallets until they were totally covered in plastic wrap. What a cool way to package boxes. Then Isaac took his pallet loader and loaded my two pallets of boxes onto his delivery truck and carted off our treasures to Carlisle's to be shipped to Boulder, CO.

While Isaac and I were doing all this work to achieve my departure on schedule, Jesse was still up in her room crying about not having a home to come back to. Jesse had such a magical time in high school with all her friends it was hard for her to leave her safe haven. The day came for me to catch my flight to Seattle and Jesse still couldn't get it together to leave her room.

I called Isaac from Boulder to let him know that Jesse was still sitting at our former home and I was no longer there. Isaac drove over with his pickup truck to inspire Jesse to get packed and move the last of her belongings over to his condo. Jesse only had a month left to stay in Alaska before she would start college in Seattle. Once Isaac got Jesse out of her former home and over to his condo she was fine. Jesse spent the month with her brother sharing her decorating and cleaning skills and helping Isaac organize his condo.

I found a lovely apartment in Boulder with a view of the Flatirons. Just across the street was a small shopping center with plenty of shops to support my lifestyle needs and help cut back on time spent in the car. I wanted to get my apartment organized before I left for Seattle at the end of the month. At the end of September I would be flying to Seattle to meet my daughter and get her moved into her dorm at the University of Washington. It was a fun week of shopping and hanging out together discovering the layout of the campus. I had promised Jesse a laptop and printer for making it through high school with top honors. Jesse had filled her dorm room with all the niceties from our week of shopping that would make her stay at college comfortable. It was a sad day when I returned to Boulder, leaving Jesse in Seattle to start college. We were both crying that day.

Starting up a new Rolfing practice is never easy. But starting up a new Rolfing practice in Boulder, where there are more Rolfers per capita than any other place in the world, is not the wisest business move I have ever made. I was just so desperate to get out of Alaska and start working on my sun deficit. Did you know that Colorado has more sunny days than San Diego? Lots of sun but no beaches or oceans. Anyway, I had already taught two Rolfing classes prior to moving to Boulder and picked up a few clients. Then Liz was so kind to send a few clients my way. Between teaching and having about 6 clients a week I almost covered my expenses. I did have a few clients in Las Vegas and would fly out once every two months staying with friends and Rolfing a little to supplement my income.

Living in Boulder with just a few clients was fun. There are plenty of things to do in Boulder, like riding the miles of bike trails

Part Two Leaving Alaska to Live in Colorado

weaving through the Boulder area. I made it my priority to ride almost every day. The scenery is breathtaking if you are hiking the Flatirons trails that butt up next to the west side of Boulder. The reason I chose Boulder to call my home was so I could be outdoors all year long. What I didn't know at the time was why the higher powers chose Boulder for me.

One of my first lessons from the higher powers begins with a simple recommendation from a friend to visit the psychic who sees angels. Boulder is the mecca of alternative realties with people who are truly psychically gifted and practitioners who pretend to be gifted. I scheduled an appointment to meet the lady who sees angels. Angel Lady was a very sweet woman and was happy to share her story of how her gift came about. She had attended church for years and out of the blue one Sunday she began to see people's guardian angels sitting with them in church. Then she began giving messages to people from their guardian angels. I'm sorry to say her husband at the time didn't like his wife's psychic gift that she had been blessed with and divorced her. Angel Lady moved away from the Midwest and of course moved to Boulder, where she could live in a place she would fit in and not be considered abnormal.

Angel Lady worked out of her home in north Boulder in a lovely dark purple room with white trim around the windows and doors. Most psychics record your session so you can go back over the reading once you return home. Angel Lady recorded my session and she was able to see my guardian angels. I have two guardian angels: one sits on my right and the other sits on my left side. The only message I could remember from the session (since I went through one of my demolition cleaning sprees in my apartment and threw out the tape) was my guardian angel told me to stop dating the current guy I had just met.

If I were to go back today I would be way more interested in what my guardian angels look like and find out what they did all day long. The Angel Lady remarked that I was psychic and wondered why I wasn't going to the psychic school in Boulder to learn more about my gift. My reply was that I used my psychic gifts in my

Rolfing practice to help my clients. 1998 was the first time I felt the presence of my guardian angels, which occurred during the first Rolfing training I taught in Boulder. The visit to the Angel Lady just confirmed their existence.

As much fun as it is to have a taste of the varied talent and scores of New Age discoveries of which you can practice, it costs money. That brings me back to my budget, which was quickly sliding my accounting to the red side of the balance sheet. Thanks to my good friend Liz, while we were out shopping one day at the Great Indoors, Liz mentioned that Sue, a Rolfer in Golden, wanted to sell her Rolfing practice to an experienced Rolfer. I didn't waste any time. As soon as I got home I placed a call to Sue. Sue and I hit it off upon our first meeting. I passed her Rolfing test by giving her a great Rolfing session. Sue wanted to make sure her clients had an experienced Rolfer before she moved back to South Carolina. Once again I had a full Rolfing practice and could start saving money. Thank you Liz, Sue, and the higher powers because my balance sheet would start showing black again.

The Visceral Training

The next Rolfing sponsored training that brought me wonderful insight into the human body was the Visceral Training with Liz Gaggini in Dec 2001. I consider Liz to be one of the most brilliant minds in the Rolfing community. Liz had studied with three of the top Visceral teachers to gain an insightful vision of working with the organs of the body. Visceral work had been done for years in Paris and was starting to catch the attention of the Rolfing community. Liz took all she had learned about working with organs and presented it with a Rolfing perspective. How do organs affect the structure of the body and once you release trauma from the organs how does it change the alignment of the structure?

How could I turn down a Visceral training on Maui? One of my best friends and Rolfing colleagues from Anchorage, Paul Van Alstine, met me at the airport in Maui. The class was held in a large house with a pool and a view from atop the foothills overlooking the ocean and Molokini Crater. The class shared the house, which helped with housing costs. The class also cooked and had group meals together, which saved on the cost of restaurant food.

In the morning we would get up early, jump in the rental car and head down the hill into Kihei for the morning walk on the beach before class. But before the walk on the beach we stopped into the health food store in Kihei for a fresh morning organic Kona coffee latte... Best way to start off the morning on Maui. It was just a short walk across the street from the health food store to the beach. In the mornings I would be sure to wear one of my sun dresses, get my Chaco's full of sand while walking on the beach, and let my eyes drink in the beauty of Maui's ocean. After our morning walk it was back up to the house on the hill to begin class. The morning classes consisted of learning the pulses of the different organs. Every organ has its own movement. Via the movement of the organ is how the organ's processes are carried out.

During our lunch break we could eat outside, take a dip in the pool, and cool off before the afternoon class. The class would sit around the pool, eat lunch and chat about the movement of organs. It was a great time to work on my tan, take in the view of the ocean, and feel the peacefulness of the island. The trade winds usually produced a cool breeze, which always felt luxurious across my skin.

The afternoon class consisted of learning to feel the organs pulse on each other. For instance, the pulse of the kidney begins by rolling in and down. Then the kidney rolls out and up. When the kidney has no pulse it is fixated and it does not process as well. We are taught to release the fixated organ and return the organ's movement back to normal.

I would like to give you an example of how effective visceral work can be. My good friend Pat, who lives in South Anchorage, (her daughter Sara is best friends with my daughter Jesse) is an RN. Her doctors recommended that she start looking for a new liver because she needed a liver transplant. I asked Pat if I could try out a visceral technique on her that I had learned in Hawaii. Since she needed a new liver I was pretty sure I couldn't cause any more damage to her liver. Pat agreed to let me try.

I was at Pat's house and didn't have my Rolfing table. So, I had Pat lay down on her living room floor. I placed one hand on the front side of her liver and placed my other hand on the back side. With a soft touch I felt for the pulse of the liver but what I found was a very swollen liver. I held Pat's liver between my hands and began to encourage a pulse to help bring the swelling down. After working on her liver for only 10 minutes I felt the liver shift. As soon as the liver shifted the swelling decreased and the liver started to feel normal under my hands. Pat sat up and said, "I can feel my liver draining. OMG my liver is draining! I can feel it." Pat went back to her doctors and they said her liver was fine but she would need her gallbladder removed.

I want to take a logical look at why the liver had become so swollen to the point of being non-functional. I believe what happened was the liver became so swollen there was no way to assess that the gallbladder was inflamed. The gallbladder was inflamed and caused the liver to swell up. But once the pressure was released from the liver and the swelling in the liver drained the doctors could assess that the gallbladder was inflamed. Happy ending, Pat got to keep her liver.

Back to the afternoon class on Maui. I had no idea that you could work on just about every organ in the body. The class learned the pulse of each organ, how to find the organ and how to release the organ's fixated pattern on each other.

The organs that we palpated were lungs, heart, kidneys, liver, spleen, pancreas, adrenals, stomach, small intestine, colon, uterus, and ovaries. That's not all the organs we palpated, but just gives you an idea of how many organs can be helped by visceral work. Organs have their own intelligence and personalities. They feel different and function differently from muscle and connective tissue. Organs respond well to practiced body workers. Sometimes when I'm working on a client's small intestine the kidney will rise up to find my fingers. The kidney is letting me know it needs work and it recognizes the healing touch. Organs have knowledge of where they should be and how they should work. If the visceral worker knows that too, then the organ knows you can help it make the changes it needs. We live in a stressful world and organs get stressed out and don't work well. They get damaged from car accidents, falls, sports and poor nutrition. The organ still works but not at 100%. That's how visceral techniques help support the health of our organs by getting them to work at their optimal level.

During the visceral training the class got one day off during the middle of the week. Let me tell you, it was a needed break for our brains and our organs. Paul and I packed our beach towels, already wearing our swimsuits and headed out the door to spend the morning snorkeling at Big Beach. We snorkeled over to a wall made up of an old volcanic flow that separated Big Beach from Little Beach to watch the big turtles catch fish. The turtles hang out by the lava flow in the water and wait for fish to be caught off guard by the waves. When the fish gets caught by the wave and slams up against the lava flow, it becomes stunned for a moment and this is what the turtle is watching for. At that moment when the fish is stunned the turtle gets its meal.

The ocean is a beautiful light blue-green and very clear for spotting the large variety of multi-colored fish that it holds. The Parrotfish is one of my favorite fish to spot, and Big Beach is a good place to see them because of their vibrant shades of turquoise, some of the most electrifying colors of turquoise I've ever seen. Second only to the turquoise is the vivid yellow on the striped angel fish.

We started snorkeling along the shore back to our beach towels. I placed my towel neatly under the shade while Paul placed his towel under the blazing sun. I'm half Scotch-Irish but that gene pool seems to dominate my appearance. I have strawberry blond hair, light turquoise eyes, and fair skin. So I'm not very well equipped to tan, but well equipped to burn. I use lots of sun block and try not to spend all day in the sun. I enjoy having my beach towel under the shade of the trees.

While snorkeling back to the beach I began to feel connected to the ocean, the beach, the sky and I understood what it was all about to be one with the planet and how all life is connected in the universe. I felt no beginning or end between the ocean and me. To feel that connection was very calming, peaceful and energizing at the same moment. I have never felt so content. Now I know why Eckhart Tolle, author of *Power of Now*, just hung out on the park bench after experiencing being connected. I contentedly sat on my beach towel and stared out at the ocean.

We had one day off from class so we drove over to Lahaina to take a look at some art galleries, do some shopping, and then have dinner. I was ready to leave the contentment of the beach and groom so I would look my best while hanging out in Lahaina. Lahaina was the first town that I had visited on the Hawaiian Islands and experienced my first series of tropical scuba dives. After diving in Hawaii I was ready to sell my dry suit and never dive in Alaska again. Growing up in Alaska, the winters are long, cold and dark, and Hawaii is one of Alaskans choice vacation spots and the closest tropical vacation destination. I have visited all the Hawaiian Islands and I love Lahaina, Maui. The green sugar cane fields sweep down from the hilltops to meet the clear turquoise ocean. Lahaina was established as a port for whalers and whaling ships during the popular use of whale oil for lamps in Europe.

Paul and I had to stop at the art gallery to see in person Christian Riese Lassen. If you have never scuba or snorkeled off the shores of Maui it is a must to see the magical way Christian captures the underwater world of brightly colored tropical fish and plants that live just below the ocean's surface. I have plenty of his post cards and one day would love to own one of his paintings.

Paul was looking for a small hand-carved pocket knife to replace the one he lost. We stopped at the knife shop and Paul began oohing and awing over the selection and types of materials and intricately carved patterns of the knife handles exhibited under the glass cases. The owner asked if we were visiting Lahaina for the first time. We shared with the owner that we were Rolfers and were taking a Rolfing training in Kihei. A lady customer overheard our conversation and shared with us that she and her husband both went to a Rolfer on the island. Her husband walked in. Both Paul and I were thinking, that's Randy Travis and his wife. They shared their stories of how Rolfing had relieved their body's pain. They just thought Rolfing was amazing.

Next on my To Do list while in Lahaina was to visit my favorite hamburger joint, a two-story open air bamboo-style building overlooking the ocean. After hours of walking along the shops I was starving. The food at the Cheeseburger in Paradise is tasty and the view priceless. Our next stop would be for dessert and the local ice cream shop has two Hawaiian flavors that I never miss out on, Hawaiian coconut and Kona Coffee, to die for. By the time I had a scoop of both I could barely move. Evenings are the best time to walk off the ice cream. Walking along the shore or on the beach you can feel the fresh warm breeze and listen to the sound of the waves lap the sandy beach and it is wonderful.

We finished out our visceral training and I'm always sad when it comes time to leave the Islands. Paul is so much fun and a close friend so it's hard to say goodbye. It's back to the Mainland to save up for the next Visceral Training Part 2.

Back in Colorado it's winter and that transition from flip-flops to ski boots felt very restrictive at first.

Bio-Tec

Boulder is full of alternative health care practices. I know quite a few Rolfers in Boulder from Rolfing workshops that I had taken over the years. The best way to find out what alternative health care works and doesn't is by asking the local Rolfers. They have a hand on the pulse of the community and anything alternative. Rolfers are a brave lot and are always looking for what works for themselves and their clients.

Cathy Griffin knew of a Bio-Tec practitioner named Gil and I was looking for a good one. Gil's Bio-Feedback machine scanned your body and made recommendations for homeopathic remedies to improve your overall physiology and health. I had been working with Gil for about a year and he had been cleaning up my immune system. The remedies he was giving me increased my energy and were helping with my allergies. My overall health was improving and once my lymphatic system was cleaned up my weight dropped to what was appropriate for my body. I was pleased with Gil's work, I was at the weight I wanted to be and I had plenty of energy at 46. I was totally enjoying my lifestyle and I was in the best shape of my life.

I had energy for my Rolfing clients (it takes lots of juice to Rolf clients). I also had energy for biking, hiking and skiing which is why I moved to Colorado. One of my clients had a sister, Barb, who loved to ski and said we should hook up and ski. Barb and I both had passes at Vail. It was not always easy to find ski buddies that had the same skill level. But Barb and I were well matched and we skied all day long across all three mountains that make up Vail. While in college my daughter would come out for Thanksgiving and Christmas. I would ski and Jesse would snowboard. It was easy for me to keep up with my 20 year-old daughter. Skiing is one of the loves of my life.

Manifesting Steamboat

I had always wanted to have my son and daughter spend a week ski vacation in Colorado with me at Christmas. The higher powers heard my wish and granted my desire because the next winter one of my clients asked if I would like to use her timeshare in Steamboat for a week for one Rolfing session. I was so excited and started cooking and putting food in the freezer for the week at Steamboat. Isaac and

Part Two — Leaving Alaska to Live in Colorado

Jesse were both in college at the time and would be able to make the trip. I picked up Isaac at the Denver Airport December 2001. We packed up the Mustang with tons of frozen food, my ski gear and Isaac's snowboarding gear, and took off the next sunny Colorado winter day for Steamboat.

Our drive to Steamboat was only 175 miles and we couldn't wait to hit the slopes. The whole family scored some great deals on lift tickets through my good friend, ski buddy and Rolfer, Keith. Keith dropped by the condo in Steamboat to ski a couple of days with Isaac and me. The condo was great with plenty of room, 2 bedrooms, 2 baths, 2 TV's, and a great kitchen so I would be able to cook all the frozen food I had brought. We made all our meals at the condo and saved mucho greenbacks. Isaac and I wanted to make sure we skied all 6 days during our stay at Steamboat.

Taking the shuttle from the condo to the mountain was very convenient. The first two days of skiing was sunny and warm with great views from the top of the mountain. After two days of skiing and boarding Isaac and I were sore. Keith suggested that we soak at Strawberry Hot Springs. The only drawback was that the road was for 4-wheel drive only, and the shuttle to the hot springs was $20 a person. That was not in my budget. So I changed up the back tires on the Mustang and headed for the hot springs at 30 miles per hour.

The road to the hot springs was snow-packed and went up and down and wound around many curves. But Isaac, Keith, the Mustang and me made it to Strawberry Hot Springs. Yes! It was a moonlit night and the location of the hot springs along the river, hidden in the forest was a magical place. I still plan to make it back to the springs during the day and take some pictures. While we were soaking our sore bodies in the hot springs and getting some relief from our play days someone yelled, "Who drove the Mustang in here?" I raised my arm and said, "I did. I'm from Alaska." It makes for good conversation with the local skiers. It was getting late and at midnight they closed down the hot springs. Let me assure you we made it back to the condo at 30 miles per hour sometime after midnight.

The soak at the hot springs was worth the trip. Isaac and I were ready for another day of skiing. I took some pictures of Isaac jumping off rock faces into the snow but we had a plastic camera and the shots showed a very small Isaac. That night we would be picking Jesse up at the Steamboat Airport. Jesse was wondering why we made her fly to Steamboat. I let her know that I was not up to driving to the Denver Airport from Steamboat. We finally found the Steamboat Airport in the dark. I think Jesse was the last person still at the airport. I couldn't understand why she couldn't see us until we got out of the car. Since Jesse started college she wore glasses and without them she couldn't see us. I had no idea her eyesight was that bad. I guess she didn't know either until she bought glasses.

With the arrival of Jesse came the snow. For the next 3 days we awoke to knee-deep powder. In the morning I would ski with Tomas and his wife Gale. Tomas is a Rolfer who trained at the RI in the class ahead of me and who now teaches at the RI. Tomas and Gale have a Rolfing practice in Steamboat. Isaac and I used to ski with Tomas and his first wife at Keystone when the area was still small and Isaac was 7 at the time.

Snowboards need a steep slope in deep powder. But skies don't need a steep slope in knee-deep powder. In the morning the powder gets all packed down and then the borders and the skiers can ski and board on the same slope.

After finishing skiing the morning powder I would meet Jesse and Isaac in the lodge for lunch and we would finish out the day skiing together. Back at the condo we had plenty of spaghetti and lasagna to eat and after skiing in powder and cold temperatures all day we were ready to eat anything in sight. All the cooking ahead of time paid off in just a few minutes in the oven and voila! Lasagna dinner by Gwin. Both Isaac and Jesse love to eat and they both love my cooking. The week in Steamboat Isaac and I skied six days in a row and by the 5th day my legs didn't hurt anymore.

At the end of the week because of all the snow the weather was below 0 at night. I was looking forward to spending Christmas with Isaac and Jesse in Boulder and seeing the sun. On the drive back we drove through a blizzard over Rabbit Ears Pass. I had snow tires but I didn't put on my chains. The top speed with chains for the Mustang is 30 mph. I was busy passing all the drivers from Texas so I wouldn't be driving 35 mph over the pass. By the time we made it through the Eisenhower Tunnel the sun began to shine. Jesse commented, "Now I see why you didn't want to pick me up at the Denver Airport."

Christmas day in Boulder the sun was out and smiling down on the three of us with 60 for the high. We hiked on snow free trails to the top of Sanitas. The view from the top of Sanitas is worth the hike. And having a sunny day for Christmas in Colorado is almost like spending Christmas in Hawaii. The trade off is snow sports instead of water sports. I was very grateful to the powers above that Isaac, Jesse and I enjoyed the ski vacation of my dreams together in Steamboat the winter of 2002.

Healer or Scammer

Back to my friend Gil that I went for the Bio-Tec, who kept after me to go see a friend of his who was a shaman. He kept telling me what a wonderful healer this person was and I should go check it out. So winter of 2003, I went to see the shaman. The shaman (who I nicknamed Dragon Lord, DL for short) wanted to trade for some Rolfing sessions. I had my first session from the shaman and I was angry for about a week. When I would Rolf DL, I would be worn out. It always amazed me that I would end up doing a 2 hour session on DL, because I only do 1 hour sessions on my clients.

That winter 2003 when Barb and I started skiing at Vail I just didn't seem to have any energy for skiing. The year before when I was skiing with Barb you couldn't get me off the mountain. But this year I just couldn't seem to keep up with Barb and Barb noticed it. She suggested I shouldn't work with this DL person during ski season so I would have some energy. I just couldn't imagine how trading sessions with DL could affect my skiing. Barb and I had planned to stay at Vail for a 3-day weekend, hangout and do some skiing. The first day of the trip I was doing good but that night I felt like I was getting a cold. No big deal, I could ski with a cold. But by the end of the second day of skiing I felt like I had picked up a really bad flu and had to go home. I have always taken very good care of myself with plenty of rest, high quality organic foods and supplements. I almost never catch a cold and if I do it doesn't last very long. But I ended up sick for a month, which turned into bronchitis and caused me to have a cough for 6 months. I have never had bronchitis in my life.

That fall of 2003 I went mountain biking in Moab for my 48th birthday with Jeff, a good friend of my son's. Jeff was going to Rolfing school and I was mentoring him in ways of seeing patterns in the body and how to affect the tissue that caused those patterns. The drive to Moab is about a 7 hour drive from Boulder, so I wanted to spend at least 3 days in Moab if we were going to spend all that time sitting in Jeff's pick-up. While driving on I-70 getting close to the turn off for Moab I could feel a shift in the energy. I knew the energy was coming from the rock formations in Moab. The closer we got the stronger I felt the energy from the rocks and land formations around the area of Moab. I was thinking this energy feels very healing. The approaching energy grid was making make me feel better.

The first day in Moab, Jeff and I obtained a guide to take us on Slick Rock. Slick Rock is a beautiful place to ride but a good place to get injured if you are not familiar with the trails. That day my cough was bad and our guide must have thought I was dying because he wouldn't let me ride the more difficult areas of the trails on Slick Rock. The next day Jeff and I ventured out on our own and took a trail that went to the top of Moab Rim. I was so happy to make it to the top as we must have been going uphill for 2 hours. To the west of Moab Rim is an amazing view of the Colorado River, and across the River you could see the infamous Poison Spider Mesa. More than one mountain biker has lost their lives there. To the northeast you have a great view of Moab and you can see across Moab to Arches National Park.

The second day while riding Moab Rim, Jeff noticed that I had hardly coughed at all during our ride. The third day we hiked to the Delicate Arch in Arches National Park. By the third day I had no cough at all. Definitely the energy in the rock formation surrounding Moab was healing. At the time I didn't realize that the energy in Moab was protecting me from DL. After my trip to Moab my energy was feeling back to normal.

Red Flag

DL seemed to be becoming a good friend of mine and I felt like I had a safe friend and shared my personal life. DL seemed like the kindest most amazing person that I had ever met. The shaman had a wonderful family. DL would buy me nice gifts and in return I felt inclined to buy DL gifts.

But some of the spiritual information that DL shared with me didn't add up. This is a warning I would like to share with any person that is working with a healer or spiritual guru. Beware when your healer becomes your best friend right away. Beware if they tell you there is no evil. That gives them liberty to take advantage of you. Beware if they tell you that no one can do anything to you if you don't want them to. They are covering their ass when bad things start happening to you. I call them life force vampires.

They want to keep you as a friend so you will keep seeing them for healing sessions, while all along they are sucking your life force during your session and you are paying them to steal your life force. Your health starts failing because they are energy vampires and you keep going to them to get better. Good people can't imagine why a healer or a spiritual guru would destroy their health by stealing their life force while paying them to do so. I had some of my clients tell me their stories of dealings with these evil, so-called healers. These so-called healers or spiritual gurus are like a black plague, and it's hard to get rid of them.

This is my story, the story of my battle with DL, an evil life force-stealing vampire.

After my first session with DL I was angry for weeks and the shaman said it would be normal for me to feel that way. After the session my small intestine hurt. I didn't look like myself. I was exhausted after each session with DL. Let me tell you, if you feel bad after a healing session you have been scammed out of your money and your health.

After working with DL once a month for a year, I began to gain weight. If you are working with a healer or spiritual guru and start gaining weight, that is a huge red flag. Your body is trying to tell you something is wrong. You may not be able to perceive that the healer is an energy vampire but your cells can feel the loss of their energy. This so-called healer wants you to think that they are helping you and they are your best friend. But that is the mask they wear so they can steal your life force energy. Your body is trying to tell you that this so-called healer has violated you. Over the years I try to think back if DL ever helped me at all. I cannot think of one instance where I was ever helped by DL's sessions. I do recall that the more I worked with DL the unhealthier I became. I was to the point in my life asking myself what happened to my life force. The joy of being alive was becoming lost to me.

I have been working in the healing business for 23 years. When my clients get done with a session with me they feel better than when they walked in the door and they are glowing with energy. You should expect that from a truly accomplished healer. The healer you pick to work with, make sure they are hooked up to the higher powers and know where their healing gifts come from.

If your healer asks if they can use your powers to heal another person, RED FLAG!!! A true healer only uses power from the light and their healing powers from the light are limitless. Any healer that asks for your energy to heal another person is not a true healer. Any healer that uses a client's energy to heal another person has lost their hook up to the light and can only steal your life force to survive. They become a black hole with insatiable energy needs. They have no conscience for the people's health they destroy. The black hole can't be healed unless that person connects back to the light. Any healer who justifies any means to accomplish their end, there is a good chance they are practicing the art of black magic. If your healer has entitlement issues they have no need for integrity because of who they think they are. They have been seduced by their ego and have lost their divine connection to the higher powers.

Christmas at Vail

The winter of 2003 my energy began to pick up after my trip to Moab. I didn't work with DL that winter. I had energy once again for skiing. Jesse came out for Thanksgiving to ski at Winter Park where we stayed one night and had dinner at the lodge. Jesse also came out for Christmas and we spent two nights in Vail. Before ending up in Vail we stopped in Silverthorne to visit Linda, my good friend and college roommate from Western State College. We spent two days with Linda skiing at Copper Mountain. I bought Jesse a new Burton snowboard so she could use it at Vail. Jesse is a beautiful snowboarder and with her new board she looked even more graceful carving turns on the slopes. I had to wear my racing skies to keep up with her. Spending Christmas in Vail was magical for me. The old main street of Vail looks like a European village with lots of snow and every building, walking bridge and tree is lit up with thousands of Christmas lights.

To reach the best part of the mountain for snowboarding for Jesse, we had to catch the gondola at Lions Head and head to the top of the first mountain. At the top of the mountain there is an ice skating rink, a lovely log cabin with Starbucks and a spectacular view of the ski runs. Vail Mountain is such a beautiful place to spend Christmas. We skied and boarded off Chair 2. Vail has some of the best velvet corduroy- groomed slopes in the world, with perfect vertical drops and sunny days for carving turns. Jesse and I agree, we love skiing at Vail.

Patty

Spring of 2004 Gil had sent me a woman client named Patty to do some Rolfing on. I was interviewing Patty trying to determine where I should start. I kept looking at Patty's face. Her face seemed to change before my eyes. One minute her face would be hers; the next moment her face would look like a young boy's, then an older lady's, then a young girl's. It wasn't the 70's anymore and I surely wasn't doing any drugs. We got through the session and Patty felt better. My small intestine felt uncomfortable, like I had eaten some bad food after working on Patty. That night it sounded like my downstairs was full of ghosts going bump in the night.

The next time I was working with Gil I ask him what was going on with Patty and shared my story of her session. So Gil calmly shared with me that Patty shared her body with about 30 entities. Great, I think about 6 of those entities live in my apartment now. That was the start of my education about entities and how they can affect people.

2004 Graduation

In June 2004 my sweetheart of a daughter Jesse graduated from UW. I was very excited, very healthy and looking forward to spending a whole week with Jesse in Seattle. Jesse and I had many girls' days out before the big day. We enjoyed shopping, facials, hair salon, and dining at great restaurants on the waterfront. Jesse wanted to look her best at graduation. Mission accomplished... she looked fabulous! Grandmother Judy and brother Isaac came down for the occasion. During her graduation I was thinking this was a fast four years, even faster than her four years of high school. It was a beautiful day sitting in the stadium looking out over a sea of caps and gowns and also being able to see the waters of Lake Washington. It was partly sunny and no drenching rains a perfect day for Jesse's graduation. My brother Paul wanted to host a graduation party at his home in Port Orchard for Jesse. Paul was more than happy to have as many of Jesse's friends over from college as she wanted. But Jesse just wanted family at her graduation party. My dad and his family were happy to join the party. Dad didn't get around well enough to watch Jesse graduate at the UW stadium,

Part Two   Leaving Alaska to Live in Colorado

but did manage to make it out to my brother's house to see her.

After the graduation ceremony Judy, Jesse, Isaac and I made a quick stop at Jesse's apartment to pick up party gifts for her and headed for the Fauntleroy Ferry. I love the ferry ride from West Seattle to Southworth. There is just something magical about driving your car on a large boat and then enjoying views of Seattle and Mt. Rainier from the deck of the ferry.

We left the ferry and were in Jesse's SUV for a short drive to Paul's long driveway. Paul and his daughters had spray painted a sign and set it in front of an old junk car that said "Happy Graduation Present". Paul, Karen, Nicole and Megan went all out decorating their home for Jesse. A large HAPPY GRADUATION banner hung over the sliding glass doors. Karen is a huge Husky's fan so there was no lack of Husky's paraphernalia decorating the house. Of course a square Husky cake sat on the table with "Happy Graduation" written in purple. Jesse was overcome with how special Paul and his family had made her graduation day. That evening the family shared Jesse's tears of joy and happiness as we all celebrated her achievement.

I did experience one strange occurrence while staying with Jesse before her graduation. Jesse and her friends were going out to party but didn't go out until midnight. I like to go to bed by midnight. In the morning they came in from partying and I woke up screaming. I had a dream that I was back in my apartment sleeping and a loud noise woke me. I was scared and began screaming. On the shuttle ride back from the airport I overheard the woman and man sitting in front of me talk of an extremely bad wind storm that occurred while I was gone. The windstorm had occurred the same night I woke up screaming in Seattle. Once I got home and went upstairs to my bedroom to unpack I noticed the damage in my closet from the wind. The wind had blown down the door from the attic onto the closet floor, including a pile of insulation. I'm sure if I had been in my bed at the time the storm hit the noise would have probably had me jumping off my bed screaming. Why would the storm affect me while I was in Seattle? All I can think was the entities from Patty that now lived in my home were scared the night of the storm and wanted me to know about it. I couldn't deal with the energy in this apartment building anymore and decided that if I couldn't get Patty's entities to move out that I was going to move myself out. These particular apartments were full of retired people and I kept feeling a death wish type of energy. I needed to move to an apartment that had a younger group of people that were busy living and not obsessed about dying.

Visualizing

I started visualizing what I wanted my apartment to look like, what kind of view it should have, how much rent I wanted to pay and it would be nice to be close to a shopping center (like I was now) that I could just walk to. I was looking all around Boulder trying to find an apartment or condo that met with my expectations. I finally looked across the street which 2 years before I had turned down an apartment downstairs. The manager showed me an apartment upstairs. I took one look and knew it was what I was looking for. The apartment was all on one floor with a great layout, 2 bedrooms, 2 full baths, a great view of the Flatirons and closer to the shopping center. The manager made me an offer below what I wanted to pay for rent that I couldn't turn down.

I'm learning if I don't get clear about what I want, I won't recognize it even when I'm staring right at it. Clarity is my secret to getting the universe to help me find or create with me who I want to be or what I want to happen during my lifetime on this planet.

The higher powers went even a step further to help me with my move. A month before my move I met Robert. Robert was so sweet and offered to help me move. He even got his friends to volunteer. I'm sure that cost him a few 6 packs of beer. Jeff, my friend and Rolfing colleague and the person I went mountain biking with in Moab, helped me move my kitchen and clothing. My good friends Carolyn and Sue cleaned up the old apartment I moved out of. I wasn't even paying attention to the calendar and a week before the move Robert asked me if I should start packing. I started packing and everything just seemed to come together. With the help of the higher powers and my friends we got me moved across the street in three days into my new visualized apartment.

A Small Plane

The summer of 2004 was a rainy one and I never thought I would enjoy the rain after living in Alaska for all those years. It's always wonderful when the afternoon showers come and cool the hot days down. My friend Robert, who helped me move, is a pilot. Robert asked me if I would like to fly in his small plane from Denver to Seattle. I love to fly in small planes and replied "When do we leave?" A small plane takes about 9 hours to fly from Denver to Seattle. So Robert asked if I had any friends that we could stay with in Montana. I had a good friend, Bob, from my advanced Rolfing class. Bob and his wife were more than happy to accommodate us.

It is much more fun going to a small airport so you can avoid the long check-in and security lines. Robert and I pull up to the hanger at Jeffco Airport where the plane was stored. Robert opened the hanger door and we pushed the plane out. We loaded our own luggage into the plane and we could bring anything we wanted. Then we climbed into the plane and taxied down the runway.

Robert has all these maps with landmarks that you watch for that acts as a double check to make sure you're flying in the right direction. In a small plane you are flying lower than a jet, have a 360 degree view outside of the plane and a closer view of the land. If you want to take a closer look at a lake or dam you can turn the plane around and take a closer look. America is a beautiful country and we flew over miles of wheat fields getting to see the less populated areas of the northwest heading towards Seattle via Montana. We would catch sight of huge grain silos and train tracks that connected the farm lands from one silo to the next.

My good friend Bob was such a sweetheart and picked us up at the Helena Airport. Bob took us to eat at a place close to the airport that he thought we would like. After our meal Bob gave us a walking tour of old downtown Helena. I fell in love with the old western town mystic. In the morning we walked into town to Bob and his wife's favorite breakfast spot.

I had stayed with Bob a couple days during the summer of 1993 after we had finished up our advanced Rolfing training. I had volunteered to take some of his stuff to Montana that wouldn't fit in his car. At the time Bob lived in Butte in an old turn-of-the-century house that was built during the height of the mining industry. My good friend Tim from Alaska had volunteered to help me drive from Denver to Seattle after I had finished my Rolfing training. The weekend Tim and I spent the night at Bob's home I had a dream of a lady that had arrived in a carriage and welcomed me into her home.

The next morning I shared my dream with Bob. Bob said it was the first owner of the house and that she liked to come visit. Bob also told me that he and some of his friends had seen her ghost before. This was my first encounter with a friendly ghost. Tim and I took the walking tour of the old mining town and it was sad to see so many of the older buildings sitting empty. Bob was working part time in Helena because his business was slow in Butte. Bob and his wife after a few years gave up on Butte and moved to Helena.

Back to the present. After breakfast Bob took us back to Helena's small airport and once Robert fueled up the plane we were off on the next leg of our journey to Seattle. The whole trip had been sunny and clear except for a few small clouds we flew through. The cool thing about flying through small clouds is you can feel the change of density in the clouds as you fly through them. When we started flying over the Cascades the cloudier it became. By the time we started our descent into Bremerton Airport it was raining and the visibility was touch and go. At times we could see the landmarks and at times we could only see clouds that were intent on touching the ground. By the time we were almost on top of Bremerton Airport

Part Two — Leaving Alaska to Live in Colorado

we could finally see the runway. I was so relieved to be standing on the ground after we landed.

My dad lives in Allen, WA, which makes him conveniently located near Bremerton Airport. My father picked us up in the pouring rain and was teasing us about carrying our rollerblades off the plane. Dad asked if the plane was to break down would we just rollerblade home?

Robert and I stayed with my daughter in her apartment in Queen Ann, the best place that she had lived during her 4 years of college at UW. Every morning Jesse and I would walk to the top of Queen Ann Hill for coffee at Starbucks, rain or shine. One morning while sitting outside of Starbucks watching the rain and people we caught a glimpse of Dave Matthews ducking into Starbucks. Isaac, Jesse and I are huge fans of the Dave Matthews Band and the three of us went to the Gorge on the Columbia River to see DMB in concert. Best sound and concert I've ever been to.

The sun came out during our visit in Seattle and so did the roller blades. Jesse, Robert and I headed out to Green Lake to enjoy the sunny day and make a few laps around Green Lake on our roller blades. The visit with the family was great but short and too soon my brother was dropping us off at the small airport for our flight back to Denver.

The trip back to Denver was much quicker than the trip to Seattle. On the way back to Denver the winds were pushing the plane along faster. The day we left Seattle the sun was out and not a cloud in the sky to be seen. The view of the ocean, Seattle and Mt. Rainier from Robert's small plane was enhancing and showed off the profound beauty of the Seattle area. At that moment I just wanted to fly a few more times around Seattle and soak up the beauty of the area.

In the fall of 2004 after Thanksgiving and before Christmas Robert ended our relationship. I found it very strange after Robert ended our relationship. I was meeting with Robert Christmas day evening so neither one of us would be alone for Christmas.

The next day when DL found out that I had spent Christmas evening with Robert, DL was angry with me. I couldn't imagine why DL would be so angry. A few days later talking to DL's friend Gil, he informed me that DL didn't like Robert at all. DL didn't even know Robert. Taking a look back I had to ask myself how could two people be so in love and have so much fun together and have such an abrupt ending. My next question to myself was, could DL have had a hand in our relationship ending so abruptly? Could DL affect that kind of change in a person's behavior?

Gifted Chiropractor

In February of 2005 I started working with a very gifted chiropractor named Jon Wall. The reason Jon was so gifted with his touch was because he could feel if the vertebrae was out of place. Jon was so specific he would adjust only the vertebrae that were out of place. It is always inspiring to work with a gifted and talented healer. Jon and I started trading out Rolfing and Chiropractic and in the process became good friends.

During the first year of our friendship Jon met Carolyn, fell in love and they married. I was happy for Jon and Carolyn. They were a great match, and I acquired another good friend, Carolyn. In the future Jon and Carolyn would be very supportive of me in my dealings with DL.

2005 Graduation

In August of 2005 my son Isaac graduated from Alaska Pacific University in Anchorage. I flew up to Alaska for the week and stayed with my good friends and Rolfing colleagues Paul and Ana. It was strange to be back in Anchorage, the city I grew up in. It had only been five years since I moved to Colorado and already I was forgetting the names of streets and where things were while driving around Anchorage. That August in Anchorage was sunny with record warm temperatures. Isaac and I spent several enjoyable days together hiking and connecting on a new level of understanding and appreciation of the parent/adult son relationship.

Plans were set with Isaac's grandparents to have Isaac's graduation celebration at their O'Malley Road home. George and Judy's home is the best place to have an outdoor barbeque especially when the days are sunny and warm. From their very large front lawn you can see the Chugach Mountains, the lake, a view of Anchorage, Cook Inlet and Mount Denali. Isaac was so excited to be surrounded and supported by his family, friends and having the most perfect day that you could wish for in Anchorage. While enthusiastically holding his graduation cake up for pictures, Isaac almost threw his cake off the cardboard.

I had a great week with my son, daughter, family and good friends in Anchorage. I was sad to be leaving my son but I had made the choice to live in Colorado with no regrets.

Friday Night Club

That fall back in Boulder I started spending time with a group called the Friday Night Club, FNC for short, a great group of local Boulder-rites, a group to cultivate new friendships with and enjoy the weekend nightlife of Boulder. I enjoyed the new friends I was getting to know. It was fun to interact with a large group of people. Richard was one of the many friends I had met that fall.

During this same period of time after having traded out work with DL for close to two years I had come to the realization that her work was not helping me but hurting my heath. I let DL know that I didn't need any more sessions. But if the shaman paid me I would still be her Rolfer, if that was agreeable. I still considered DL to be my friend and still shared my personal life of having friends within the FNC.

Unknown to me a strange chain of events began to unfold after I informed DL that I had no need of the healing sessions. The first link in this strange chain of events was what happened to my friend Richard (who I started calling Dragon Boy, DB for short) from FNC.

DB began to fall madly in love with me. For my part in this romantic endeavor, well there was no part for me because I only thought of DB as a friend. DB and I still were friends and would see each other now and then. The strangest thing, I found myself being attracted to DB but I knew I wasn't attracted to him. Oh!!!! I started thinking something is not right here. Was DB using some kind of love spell on me? DB had talked to me about studying with a shaman in Tahiti and that he had special healing gifts. By this time I was thinking DB was the bad guy in my life movie and kept him at a distance.

For Thanksgiving I was planning a four-day ski vacation in Winter Park that included a large turkey from Whole Foods already cooked with all the fixings. My daughter and friend would be joining me from Seattle with snowboards in tow. Paul and Anna from Alaska also would be joining us. The first two days of skiing were great…sunny and the snow conditions were good with lots of runs open.

Well, I felt sorry for DB because he didn't have anywhere to go for Thanksgiving, so you guessed it, I invited him for dinner. What was I thinking? I wasn't! DB had dinner with us and then stayed. He didn't want to ski, but wanted me to hang out with him all day sitting around drinking coffee. I am not a sit around person or a coffee drinker. I went skiing with my friends and daughter. Of course DB left in a huff because no one wanted to babysit him. My legs started cramping up on me that day but thanks to Advil I finished the last day of skiing with style. The holiday ended and Jesse went back to Seattle and my friends went back to Alaska.

I had worked so hard that summer to get in shape for skiing and I was so looking forward to the winter ski season. But after the Thanksgiving holiday I ended up being sick the rest of the winter and unable to ski. I'm wondering what in the world is going on? One

Part Two — Leaving Alaska to Live in Colorado

day I felt perfectly fine and the next day I went into decline for the rest of winter. I started thinking that DB was the cause of me being sick, but the how and why was out of my realm of reality for the time being. I started asking my guides for help to see what was truly going on in my life.

During that winter I saw Gil, who began treating my symptoms with homeopathic remedies and I started feeling much better. My good friend and amazing ski buddy Barb invited me to stay with her in Vail at her relative's condo in Lion's Head for spring skiing. The condo is a wonderful place to stay and just a short walk to the gondola. Barb and I drove to Vail, unloaded the car and carried our stuff to the condo. I knew that I brought my homeopathic remedies. I remembered placing the bottle in the outside pocket of my back pack but I was unable to find the remedies after I emptied the car. I started to panic a little bit because if I didn't find them by tomorrow I was going to start feeling like shit. That day on the mountain was cold, windy and the snow was hard as a rock. I fell that day on the hard snow pack; I never fall skiing and if I do I know how to fall so I don't injure my body. For the first time ever I landed on my elbow and jammed my humerus into the shoulder joint and damaged the cartilage. That incident pretty much ended my three-day ski weekend at Vail.

As I was packing my car to head back to Boulder I found my glass bottle of remedies. They had rolled under the seat during the unpacking of my Mustang. So as I was driving to Boulder I called my friend Keith who is a Rolfer and Acupuncturist. The pain in my shoulder was growing more intense with the continued swelling of the joint. Lucky for me I caught Keith at home and he so kindly let me come to his house. Once I reached Keith's abode my shoulder was screaming. Keith pulled out his Acupuncture needles and placed them in AP point of the surrounding muscle groups of the joint. After Keith's placement of about 50 needles or so the pain and swelling in my shoulder subsided. I was very grateful for Keith's kind healing ability.

I headed home feeling sorry for myself because I was missing another weekend of skiing at Vail. That night I was lying in bed wondering what the hell just happened to me that day. I'm thinking to myself, "Am I starting to see a pattern here? Someone or some energy doesn't want me to be skiing. Why would anyone not want me to ski? Could DB be the reason for a sabotaged spring ski weekend?"

My Brother's Visit

That April, my brother Paul and his daughter Nicole came for a visit to try some alternative healing techniques. Paul had seen Gil before (the same person that made homeopathic remedies for me). So Paul wanted his daughter to see Gil too to help her deal with anxiety and also my friend Judy Cardell, a therapist that counsels clients dealing with anxiety. Nicole's visit went well with Gil, and the counseling session with Judy gave Nicole tools to deal with her anxiety.

After Paul's busy morning with remedies and counseling he had scheduled a Rolfing session for the afternoon. I had learned to feel people's aura from DL. There is an energetic field around the body that's created by the heart. So before I started the Rolfing session I checked Paul's aura to see how strong his energy field was around his body. Most auras I can feel a foot away from the body. When a person is healthy and in a good mood I can feel their aura two feet around the entire body. When I checked my brother's aura I could feel no energy around his body at all.

My brother had been under a lot of emotional stress during this visit. I was thinking how could I get his energy up without draining my own energy? I had been investigating the healing energy of crystals and I could feel the energy the crystals possessed when I held them in my hands. Crystals also have an aura around them that I can feel. The bigger the crystal the stronger the aura is around it and the farther its radius extends around the crystal. I had been collecting a few crystals since I had moved to Boulder. I went through my apartment gathering up every crystal that I could find and put them under my Rolfing table. Then I felt for my brother's aura once again. I was delighted and amazed that the crystals under the table were charging up Paul's aura. I was able to feel a six inch aura around my brother's body. Yes! Now I had some energy to work with.

When I'm Rolfing clients, they always leave with more energy than they came in the door with. But the client needs to come in with some energy for me to work with. That's why I don't work on clients when they are sick because there's not enough energy to change the tissue. If a client has enough energy to change tissue and I improve the alignment of the tissue and structure the client's energy increases. In the case of my brother his emotional distress was stressing his heart and decreasing his body's ability to generate the aura around his body. The crystals under my Rolfing table recharged Paul's heart. In turn I was able to change the tissue to increase his energy. At the finish of Paul's session his aura had increased to a foot away from his body.

At the end of the session my brother stood up, noticed a huge difference in his energy and felt much better. Before the session Paul had taken his remedies from Gil that morning but hadn't noticed any changes. The last visit Paul had made to Gil's he noticed the effect of the remedies right away. Now that Paul's energy was up after the Rolfing session with the help of the crystals he could feel the remedies start to work. For good health I feel it is essential to keep your energy up so your body can work at its optimal level.

That was the day I discovered the healing power of crystals. I have become a big fan of the Gem and Mineral Show that comes to Denver once a year. The Gem and Mineral Show helps buying larger crystals affordable. Over the years the crystals under my table have gotten larger which increases the energy available for my clients' tissue, making my job of changing tissue easier.

Dragon Boy

After avoiding DB for almost a year, I ran into him at the St. Julien

Hotel. Instead of leaving before DB caught sight of me, we were engaged in polite conversation before I could run away. I'm not gifted at confrontational conversation, especially when I have no idea what I am dealing with. DB bought me a drink and we danced a while. So I'm thinking so far so good. I liked having DB for a friend; he seemed to be a sweet person.

Then as we were leaving the dance floor DB placed his hand on my back and the pain in my kidneys almost brought me to my knees. It didn't take any more encouragement for me to get the hell out of the St. Julien and away from DB.

The next week I didn't feel much better. I made an appointment with DL. I showed up for the session and the energy felt strange. The house was full of energy that felt like swirling dancers all around me. I felt like I had picked up some type of spirit or bad energy from DL. I was hoping that DL could rid me of the pain and whatever type of energy I had picked up from DB. As always with the sessions with DL my small intestines hurt and would swell up, and I remembered the reason why I didn't come to DL for sessions anymore. It seemed to me that I had picked up more negative energy than I walked in the door with.

In my desperation for some type of relief from my pain and trying to regain some of my energy back, I scheduled an appointment with Gil. Thank goodness for Gil. He was able to make some remedies to rid me of all the entities that I had picked up from my encounters with DB and DL. After taking the remedies I started to feel my energy increase. My brain was racing around in confusion. Apparently I picked up entities from DL and DB and that's why my small intestines hurt every time I went for a session with DL or was around DB and he touched me. For some reason I was still Rolfing DL and afterwards I would be exhausted and my small intestines would hurt. I would ask myself why I kept Rolfing DL. The answer to that question always seemed to escape my thought process somehow.

Part Two Leaving Alaska to Live in Colorado

At the end of October 2006 I was still in such a cloud of confusion I was at a loss of what I could do. I prayed a lot to the higher powers for help and guidance. I'm always amazed how my prayers are answered. I don't always realize at the exact moment my prayers are being answered but sooner or later I see results.

My Friend

An old friend from Alaska, Tim Saunders, was going to a raw food potluck in Aspen and wanted to know if he could stay at my place a few days in Boulder. He also wanted to know if I was interested in a three day ski trip to Aspen. I had never skied Aspen and I was very excited for the chance to see that part of Colorado. Tim and I shared a longstanding spiritual relationship spending many hours discussing the *Power of Now* by Eckhart Tolle. You could say we were on the same spiritual page.

It was so good to see Tim, as it had been about eight years since we spent any time together. It was good to have someone to talk to about all the strange things that were happening in my life. The best part was Tim didn't think I was a nut case. Tim shared with me the strange encounter he had with a woman that he dated in Florida. She was able to get him to do things that he normally wouldn't consider. She got him to deposit $10,000 in a joint checking account; then proceeded to spend the entire $10,000 and asked for more. Tim started to suspect there was something more going on here than what he could perceive.

This woman had talked to Tim about her ex-husband's participation in black magic. Tim found out this woman was practicing black magic, too. She told Tim of rituals that she had participated in with a coven. At the time Tim didn't think that black magic existed. But once he got out of the relationship he started to suspect there was more to black magic than he had ever imagined.

Then we started to ask the pendulum questions about black magic and if it could be affecting our behavior or sucking our life force energy. Neither one of us was happy with the answers we were getting about black magic. I couldn't imagine that sweet DL would be using black magic. The shaman treated me like a best friend and seemed so sweet, caring and kind. All the things that were happening to me weren't adding up. For Tim it made total sense, the things that woman got him to do and to his amazement he did them

willingly. The woman had used black magic on him to control his behavior. What could we do to protect ourselves from black magic? We had no clue but the search for answers was set into motion.

The first weekend that Tim spent with me in Boulder was Thanksgiving and I had planned a skiing holiday weekend at Winter Park. My Rolfing colleague, Bridge, offered to let me use his parent's condo in Winter Park for a few Rolfing sessions. The condo in Winter Park was homey and had a gas fireplace…very cozy. I was having trouble skiing and wasn't feeling like I had any energy. When I'm skiing the only thoughts I usually have are about skiing. But for some reason DL kept popping up in my mind. That was the last person I wanted to think about. It was ruining my day of skiing and throwing off my concentration. The next thing I knew I fell and injured my left shoulder. My right shoulder had just gotten better from the fall I had at Vail the year before. Two years in a row I managed to injure both shoulders. I'm an expert skier and for the last 40 years of skiing I had never injured either shoulder.

I had never been so distracted from skiing and never felt so drained of energy for no apparent physical reason that I could see. My life was at an all time low of having no energy. The things I enjoyed most in life I didn't have the energy for like I had before I started working with DL. Still I couldn't see the big picture of why or how DL or any person could be affecting my life in such a destructive manner.

Before we drove the next weekend to Aspen I had a dream about a huge snowstorm. Instead of driving the Mustang we rented an SUV. I was so glad we weren't in the Mustang because Aspen was getting dumped on the night we arrived at our lodging in Buttermilk. After unpacking I noticed my energy began to increase.

Part Two — Leaving Alaska to Live in Colorado

My red eyes started looking more normal and the whites of my eyes hadn't looked this good in a couple of years. My mind wasn't being pounded with thoughts of DL.

Friday we skied at Aspen Mountain and I was starting to feel like my old energetic self again. I had a great day of skiing with no thought in my head except to enjoy the 2 feet of fresh snow and the sunshine on my face.

We did encounter a spirit that was staying in our condo that evening which asked for our help. The spirit told us of his great love he had for his betrothed. He had a mining claim on the river which would make him a wealthy man. And as soon as he had made enough money he vowed to marry this great love of his and start a family. Sadly enough, one day while working his claim on the river, four claim jumpers killed him and dumped his body in the river. He was never angry about his murder but was consumed by the knowledge that his betrothed never knew what happened to him and no one ever acknowledged his death. So we asked our spirit guides to give a message to his great love and tell her what had happened to him. Then we visualized putting two dozen roses at the river site where he had died. Finally his spirit was at peace and he was able to cross over to the light.

Snowmass was our next ski area to check out. I loved skiing at Snowmass. I never thought I would enjoy a ski area more than Vail. I had another great ski day with only thoughts of skiing and my energy stayed good. That evening we started back to Boulder enjoying a beautiful drive through Glenwood Canyon, still light out, watching the full moon peek at us above the canyon walls. My energy was better, but after Tim flew back to Alaska I started feeling my energy drain away with no understanding of what was affecting it.

Drive to Seattle

In 2006 my daughter was hosting her first Christmas dinner at her home in Seattle. My son would also be flying down from Alaska to celebrate the holiday season with us. Most winters in Boulder are very mild with not much snow. But not this winter…it snowed every Thursday (my day off) for eight weeks in a row! Instead of the Weather Channel reporting only a few inches per snow fall it began reporting 2 to 4 feet per snowfall!

On the Thursday I was to leave on my flight for Seattle the snowfall turned to a blowing snowfall, which shut down the Denver Airport. I tried to reschedule my flights but none were available until December 27th and that totally didn't work for getting me to Seattle for Christmas. It was December 21st, only 4 more days until Christmas. Thinking to myself: I don't want to stay here and have my energy drained by DB. Then I had this compelling urge to drive to Seattle in the Mustang, so I called my daughter to let her know I was driving. Jesse didn't want me driving in winter weather conditions. But I couldn't miss Jesse's first Christmas in her house or miss seeing my son for Christmas.

I packed up the Mustang and left the 21st of December at 4 o'clock in the evening driving I-70, the only road that wasn't closed leaving the state of Colorado. I had planned to drive all night and talk with Jesse and Tim on my cell phone. While driving past Idaho Springs I was talking to Jesse and she asked me if I had a car charger for my cell phone. It was on my list to buy but I hadn't bought it yet. Oops, a slight oversight on my part. It was still early and I hoped that I could find a charger at the Target store in Silverthorne. A cell phone is not much use when the battery is dead. Around 6 pm I reached Target, never so happy in my life that Silverthorne had a Target and it was open. I found the phone chargers but couldn't find the one for my phone. Then a sales person showed up and found the right charger for my phone. I was so grateful to find the charger because without it, it would have been a very long night with no one to talk to. My guardian angels were surely looking after me that evening. I'm also blessed with an extremely smart daughter. My daughter was relieved to hear that I had found a phone car charger in Silverthorne.

Part Two — Leaving Alaska to Live in Colorado

The great thing about driving at night is there is no traffic and with all the heavy snowfall on the sides of the road it was much easier to see in the dark. When you drive through Salt Lake City at 5 am commuting is a breeze. So I'm making good time, talking to Tim and Jesse on the phone while they are keeping me awake. If I can keep up this driving pace I will make it to Seattle in 24 hours. Once I hit the Utah/Idaho border I started to encounter a few snow flurries but my pace is still good. Then after about 50 miles into Idaho I'm driving in a full-fledged blizzard in about 6 inches of snow in my vehicle of choice, a Mustang.

I'm out in the middle of nowhere Idaho with a full tank of gas with no chance of getting off the highway. Even if I did get off the highway I would be stuck in the snow with absolutely no chance of getting back on the highway. Stick it out or freeze. Lucky for me I was behind a white Chevy Yukon. The Yukon was breaking trail through the snow so I stayed right behind it until dawn so I could keep from getting stuck in the snow. I didn't want to end up another traffic statistic in the snow bank.

By dawn I was about half way through the farm lands of Idaho. The snow had let up and the depth of the snow was diminishing the farther I drove toward my destination. That was a good thing because I needed to get more gas and the depth of the snow was a determining factor of whether I could navigate the off and on ramps to the oasis truck stops. I was ecstatic when I pulled into the truck stop and was able to fill up my almost empty gas tank, visit the loo and get a bite to eat. I had just spent 2 hours driving in a blizzard but the snow had stopped and the sun was breaking through the clouds. Easy sailing from here on out, I thought, only 2 hours to Boise. But halfway to Boise the sun was shining, the wind was blowing the snow across the road, the highway had turned to glare ice and the SUV's were sliding off the road right and left. And I'm still driving the Mustang, OMG! I drove on what was left of the snow pack at the left edge of the fast lane to get some traction.

I did get better traction but had to keep my speed up to keep driving in the fast lane. Passed a bad accident with multiple vehicles off the highway in a field. As I drove by an officer gave me a very angry look for driving too quickly past the accident. Rule of thumb, never step on your breaks while driving on glare ice. The best I could do was to take my foot off the gas pedal to slow down. I get past the officer and hope he doesn't give me a ticket. Perhaps the officer decided that chasing after a car he thought passed by an accident too quickly on glare ice wasn't such a good idea after all.

If driving on glare ice isn't stressful enough, as I'm driving along SUV's are still sliding off the road in front of me. The wind is blowing across the highway and the wind is starting to blow my car toward the snow bank. I'm trying to stay calm, keep my foot off the brake and whatever I do I mustn't make any sudden corrections with the steering wheel. Very slowly I incrementally correct the direction of the Mustang back to the center of the lane. A few times my car would start to lose traction and fishtail, so I would just take my foot off the gas and the Mustang would straighten out.

By some miracle I managed to make it to Boise that morning. My guardian angels must have been on both sides of my car keeping it on the glare ice. Then Denny's caught my attention because I was starving, needed to visit the loo, and wanted to stand up after sitting in the Mustang for 2 stress-filled hours. As I sat and ate a tasty breakfast trying to recover from my driving ordeal and gain some energy from my meal, I was hoping I could still make it to Seattle by nightfall. As I was talking to my daughter that morning on the phone I'm sure she was happy to hear, I was still headed toward Seattle.

"On the road again" become my motto for this road trip. After a short break in Boise I was on the road again. The sun was warm and bright, the snow was melting, the road started to dry up, and I began to make up the time I had lost during the snowstorm and my encounter with ice driving. I was doing great, only 150 miles from Seattle. It was 4 pm and I had now been driving for 24 hours. Then I hit thick fog. That's when I lost it. I called my son and told him I couldn't drive any longer. Isaac told me to stop and get a hotel. So I stopped in Kennewick and stayed the night.

I didn't want to stop for the night since I was trying to out run a storm that would be moving through Snoqualmie Pass after midnight. Once I had dinner, got comfortable on the bed and watched some TV I was thinking about driving the rest of the way to Seattle that night. If there hadn't been the fog to contend with I would have made it to Seattle that night. The next morning Snoqualmie Pass had stop-and-go traffic and the fog was still thick. My brother suggested I back track a little and drive to Portland to avoid the pass. Once I headed for Portland the fog cleared out and the drive to Seattle was 6 hours instead of 3. The roads were clear the rest of my drive. After 30 hours of driving and one night's rest I made it to Seattle by Saturday the 23rd of December, thanks to the higher powers for making sure I survived my cross-country quest to be with my daughter and son for Christmas.

I was ever so happy that I wasn't in my car anymore, once I made it to Jesse's house. I was so excited that I was able to help Jesse fix her first Christmas dinner. Yes! I made it to Seattle before Christmas. Isaac was very excited about eating Jesse's first Christmas dinner. His two most favorite meals of the year are Turkey Day and Christmas. The prime rib was cooked to perfection. It was a stunning first meal for Jesse's first Christmas dinner. Isaac, Jesse and I all live so far apart it had been five years since the last time the three of us were together for Christmas. It's always a very special Christmas when I get to spend it with my son and daughter.

My brother's daughter Nicole, 16 years of age, wanted to drive back with me to Seattle. I'm sure she would have liked to drive the Mustang but the road conditions weren't the best for beginning drivers. I can't think of any reason why anyone would want to go on a road trip in the middle of the winter. But whatever her reasons were I was very grateful for her volunteering to make the drive back to Denver with me. Since Nicole was driving back with me to Denver my brother let me know up front that he didn't want me driving round the clock. I was more than happy to make our trip in 3 days and sleep over two nights.

The weather was clear and sunny for the first 2 days of the drive back, no blizzards or ice driving. I defiantly wanted to keep my precious cargo safe and sound on our winter road trip. Only once did I forget to take the fuel hose out of the gas receptacle of the Mustang while driving away from the gas pump.

When you spend 3 days in a car you have a lot of time to talk about whatever you want to talk about. Nicole and I had plenty of stories to share. Nicole told me of a dream she had come true when she was a small girl. As she got older, she talked of being able to see spirits in her room coming from downstairs where her grandmother lived. She was so happy to share this information with someone who also had spiritual gifts. Nicole shared with me she hadn't told her parents of what she had dreamed of or the spirits she had seen in her room. Nicole didn't think they would understand what she was experiencing or believe her.

The second day was a long day because we wanted to make it to Glenwood Springs for a soak in the hot springs. We made it there by 8 and checked into the Springs Hotel because we didn't have time to find another hotel if we wanted to get a soak in before the springs closed by 9. If you stayed at the Springs Hotel the price of the hot springs was included. So we checked in and made a mad dash for the springs.

We enjoyed the hot springs for almost an hour before they made everyone leave. The hot springs took the pain out of my joints after driving the Mustang for 12 hours. It was a hot shower and the both of us were asleep before we could spend any time talking.

I had thought of driving home after our soak in the hot springs. But while Nicole was taking her shower at the Springs Hotel, I was watching the news when the weather came on: a blizzard on the other side of the tunnel; expecting 3 to 4 feet of snow. Lucky for me I was sitting on the bed watching the weather and not driving in it. I had had enough blizzard driving for this holiday.

Part Two — Leaving Alaska to Live in Colorado

The next morning was one of those beautiful sunny days in Colorado with bright blue skies for our drive back to Boulder with dry roads on this side of the tunnel. Nicole and I felt quite refreshed after a soak in the springs and a sleep where you don't move a muscle all night long. The 3rd day of this road trip would be a short drive, only 176 miles left to go. We made good time to the tunnel but once we reached the east side of the Eisenhower Tunnel there was 4 feet of snow on the east side of I-70. The road was snow packed with potholes here and there. The traffic was moving along at a quick pace for the road conditions and I was moving right along with everyone else in a hurry to get home. Nicole was delighted by the immense amounts of snow and started taking pictures at any bathroom breaks we took along the way. The snow was a sparkled vision of white. But I was busy keeping my eyes on the road, watching the SUV's slide off the road and was unable to take a closer look at all that snow.

The driving that day was challenging but not as bad as compared with driving through Idaho farmland. We arrived in Golden with only 22 miles left to go. I had never seen the snow so deep on Highway 93 (the road between Golden and Boulder) and looking like a glimmering desert of white, intensified by the bright shining sun reflecting back the light that stretched on for miles. Nicole had never seen so much fresh snow and was once again taking pictures of Colorado's winter wonderland. Finally my home was in sight and the toughest part of the drive was getting from the plowed road through a unplowed road into my carport. Nicole thought it was great fun watching me bound around the deep snow rutted street in the Mustang to make it to the safety of my carport. I was thinking, this can't be good for my muffler.

Nicole and I had 3 days of hanging out in Boulder. Nicole loves to visit the Pearl Street Mall and wanted to see if any of the street performers were willing to brave the cool or the snow today. No street performers could be found that day we were at the Mall. We just had to settle for shopping at the crystal shop and enjoy a hot latte. El Loro is where I buy most of my crystal jewelry and drag any family members to see when they come for a visit. For Nicole it's one of her favorite shops in Boulder. Of course there is a Starbucks across the street from El Loro, perfect for warming up your whole body with a Starbucks coffee. Before I could wonder how 3 days passed so quickly I was taking Nicole to the Denver Airport for a short two and a half hour flight back to Seattle.

Looking back on my road trip to Seattle made me realize how desperate I was to leave Boulder. Once I had time to think, after Nicole's departure, I noticed how my energy had come up and I wasn't feeling so stressed out. Even though I was driving at night on my road trip to Seattle, after I was about 100 miles from Boulder my energy began to increase and I didn't feel so agitated. I was thinking that DB was an energy vampire and when my energy was being sucked out of my body I would become agitated. The whole time I spent with my family in Seattle I had plenty of energy and I felt like my old happy self again.

Staying in Touch

Tim and I stayed in touch during the end of December and all of January. We spent many hours talking on the phone wondering about answers to questions we weren't sure how to even ask. Tim always listened to an off-the-beaten-path radio station that hosted a guest speaker named Raymon Grace. He taught a class every year in Boulder about dowsing. Raymon's class included a wide array of hands-on methods. The process taught students how to use the pendulum. He talked about changing energy and getting rid of life force sucking spirits or entities. Tim planned on taking Raymon's class in Boulder in August to acquire some defensive tools. In the meantime Tim ordered Raymon Grace's book that January.

I had been using a pendulum for years and Tim wanted me to teach him what I knew of dowsing. In February Tim traveled back to Boulder for an extended period of time to learn how to protect himself from the black magic that still plagued him from his ex-girlfriend and also help me deal with Dragon Boy who I thought might be using black magic on me to drain my energy. As the saying goes, two heads are better than one. So why not combine our energy to continue the on-going spiritual battle of light against the darkness.

Tim showed me an article he had pulled off the Internet about energy vampires. The author of the article had pictures of people's auras. He showed what normal healthy auras looked like and what kind of damage energy vampires cause to the aura. The author talked about how staying around an energy vampire would eventually deplete the victims to the point of illness or death. I had been having problems with my energy being depleted since I had started trading out with DL four years earlier. I started to realize that DL was an energy vampire. For some reason I couldn't fathom at that insightful moment why I still didn't end our friendship. I also recognized that Dragon Boy was an energy vampire but I managed to stay away from that life force draining person.

Tim suffered a shoulder injury a year earlier pulling wire through conduit. Tim had worked in Alaska for years as a master electrician. He had been to quite a few therapists in Alaska but his shoulder was not getting any better. Tim's injured shoulder added another reason to the list of why he came to Colorado for an extended visit. Tim had been a Rolfing client of mine for 10 years earlier when I had a Rolfing practice in Alaska.

During our conversations on the phone I assured Tim that I had restored many of my clients' injured shoulder joints to 100%. For compensatory issues with Tim's injury I had Tim see my chiropractor, Jon Wall, to help open the vertebral joints in the upper thoracic spine. When Tim had first showed up at my door in Boulder he could barely raise his arm to put on his jacket without his shoulder causing him extreme pain. With my Rolfing combined with Jon's chiropractic treatments, Tim's shoulder and upper thoracic spine were improving quickly.

I had this great idea that Tim should see DL. I wonder who put that great idea into my head. Then I could get his take on how it felt for him to get worked on by DL. Tim went for his session with DL and it sounded like it was a complete disaster. At the beginning of Tim's session with DL, DL was wondering why I was not there. DL seemed to be very angry that I was not there. Tim was not impressed with DL's demeanor and didn't feel like the session helped him in any healing manner. Tim felt DL conducted the session in a very unprofessional manner considering DL had been a practicing shaman and healer for years.

DL didn't say much to me about Tim after his session. Tim assured me that DL didn't care for him. DL didn't seem to like any man that I was friends with or dated. Why would DL dislike all of my male friends? Why would DL treat a client so poorly that I recommended?

Boy, did we both suffer a lot of pain after Tim's session with DL. We were still thinking that Tim's ex-girlfriend and DB were practicing the dark arts on us. We were reading Raymon Grace's book and it explained how to change energies with the pendulum and it seems to be helping. Tim and I have been hiking almost 3 or 4 times a week but I was having severe pain in my knees, the kind of pain that feels like someone is poking the bone with a large needle. To deal with the knee pain I just doubled up on my joint supplements.

Spring rolled around and Tim and I started getting bit by brown recluse spiders. Brown recluse spiders are very poisonous. Clients of mine who have been bitten by them end up in the hospital on steroids and antibiotics. Then if the bite goes too long before treatment the doctor will cut out the infected part of the skin that is bitten. I'm a big fan of 35% hydrogen peroxide and always keep some in my fridge. I have used 35% H2O2 on wasp bites; it oxidizes the venom. I tried H2O2 on the recluse bites and it oxidized the venom and the bite healed within a few days. I'm thinking I have the brown recluse spider's number and we shouldn't be getting bit anymore.

Part Two — Leaving Alaska to Live in Colorado

Within a couple of weeks Tim ends up with 4 or 5 bites on the inside of his leg before he realizes they are brown recluse bites. The inside of Tim's leg was starting to look bad by the time we started treating it with H2O2. But the venom was destroyed and the inside of Tim's leg started healing. By the time Tim's leg was healed I got bit 4 or 5 times on my back. I couldn't see the bites and Tim couldn't tell that I had been bit. After about a week I experienced pain at the bite sights and felt pain down my arm. I started to realize that I had been bitten again. I started using the H2O2 on my back but I was losing the strength in my arm and I knew the venom was affecting the nerves.

I also just happen to have a Rife machine, which is a machine that produces different frequencies. Every living organism, bacteria, virus, or venom has a certain frequency. I used the brown recluse frequency to oxidize the venom in the nerve that was affecting my arm. The pain went away and the strength came back in my arm right away using the Rife machine 10 minutes at a time for 3 days. After being viciously attacked by the recluse spiders we started treating anything that appeared to look even slightly like a spider bite. We were still getting bit now and then. But now I was killing any spider on sight no matter what color it was.

By July I'm starting to think that this can't be normal behavior for spiders. Got to love Google. I googled BRS: they are reclusive and don't bite humans unless their hiding place is disturbed. We searched every inch of my apartment and found no spider nests. But I did discover that the decorative pine trees outside my bedroom window and Tim's bedroom window were prime lodging for BRS. I decided that these spiders were being compelled to bite us. So whoever was compelling the spiders to bite us was using black magic to get the job done.

In August Tim and I flew to Seattle for my father's 80th birthday party. Even though my father's birthday is actually October 25th, my brother planned to celebrate Dad's birthday in August to avoid the rainy season in Seattle. Summer in Seattle is the perfect weather for the whole family to travel to Washington for a 3-day barbeque to celebrate 80 years of an amazing life that our dad has lived.

Once again I noticed I had more energy while I was in Seattle with my family. Both Tim and I seemed to be unaffected by all the black magic that was haunting us in Boulder. I had a carefree week spending time with the family. Jesse, Megan and I were sun bathing on the deck of my brother's boat. We watched my brother, Tim and my son take turns water skiing behind the boat. The family got together and checked out the car show in Port Orchard. After the car show we took the ferry from Port Orchard back to my daughter's home in West Seattle. My daughter and I had time to take a walk around Green Lake. When Isaac and Jesse spent the summer at Grandpa's house we would walk to Green Lake, play in the water and eat our picnic lunch on the lawn. My dad had the best 3-day 80th birthday celebration. Isaac must have taken 300 pictures. I printed up a photo book of Dad's celebration with his picture on the cover. Before I knew it the week was over.

After flying back to Boulder the painful attacks on our bodies started up again and the life force from our bodies was being drained once again. We were still being bit by the brown recluse spider. But in the spring, the BRS bites were lessening because I bought praying mantis to eat the BRS. The praying mantis seemed to be working quite well.

Finally, the end of August arrives, the day Tim and I have patiently been waiting for Raymon Grace's class on dowsing. Tim loved Raymon's class and all the information he gained supported us in battling the strange things that had been happening to us. After class Tim shared everything he had learned in class with me. Then we took the information and started using it to clear the energy of black magic by shifting energy with our pendulums.

One of Tim's classmates shared a book with him about clearing entities. The book is *Shaman Healer, Sage* by Alberto Villoldo, who is learning from a shaman in the Peruvian mountains. This book was a turning point in our understanding of entities and how they

Part Two   **Leaving Alaska to Live in Colorado**

can cause pain in people's bodies. Another huge fact we learned, just because you don't believe in shamans doesn't keep them from affecting you; they can still cause you pain and illness. If a spirit or entity sets up housekeeping in your body they can cause you pain and the reason you are feeling pain is the entity is stealing your life force so they can survive in your body. A spirit can be a deceased relative who is afraid to cross over. The spirit is unaware of the damage it is causing to their living relative host. Tim and I learned that you can explain to the spirit the damage they are causing in their host and help them cross over to the light. These spirits are very cooperative. Some spirits don't want to leave and are much harder to evict from the body.

   The next step of our journey into the spirit realm was to learn how to rid ourselves of spirits who don't what to leave the physical realm. In the doctor's book he talks about clear quartz crystals and how spirits are attracted to them. Crystals are a great tool for pulling spirits out of a person's body. Luck was with us and soon after Tim finished Raymon's dowsing class the yearly Gem and Mineral Show started in Denver the 3rd weekend of September. Bright and early Saturday morning we were standing in line for the Gem and Mineral Show. Never having been to a gem and mineral show before I had no idea what we were getting ourselves involved in. If you do decide to visit the Gem and Mineral Show bring lots of money. The types, shapes and sizes of crystals that were available to buy overwhelmed me, from a small bobble costing only a few dollars to giant crystals that you could feel their energy from across the room costing thousands of dollars.

   When I walked in the door of the Gem and Mineral Show I had a short list of crystals to buy. I wanted an amethyst, a purple stone for healing to put under my Rolfing table, and a clear quartz crystal ball. The fortune tellers always had one and though I had no idea what I would do with a crystal ball, I knew I just had to have one. Then we found the crystal beads. Beads we could make necklaces for protection from black magic or negative energies. We spent all day going from one exhibit to the next and I made a few trips to the

ATM. I found a beautiful crystal ball from Madagascar. I also found a dark colored amethyst with large formed crystals from Brazil.

This finished off most of the money I had brought. So many sparkly pretties to buy but I was sticking to my budget. The important aspect of our shopping adventure accomplished, we now had clear quartz crystals, the reason we had come to the gem show. I had a whole year to save money for the next gem show and I was making my list.

Once we filled my apartment with crystals you could feel the space become clearer and feel more energy in the apartment. When we both became chilled, started to experience pain or just felt agitated we knew it was time to pull out the clear quartz and begin clearing the apartment of entities. First Tim and I would use the pendulum to call on the higher powers to clear the room and fill the clear quartz with entities or spirits. After the room was clear we used the pendulum again and called on the higher powers to help all entities and spirits cross over to the other side and out of my apartment. When all the other negative world energy was cleared from the apartment we would both warm up, feel our energy increase, our pain decrease and we would be back to our happy positive selves.

Rose quartz crystals became the next crystal we started buying. On one of our crystal hunts we turned off Highway 24, the road that heads to Pike's Peak. Right after you turn off 24 there is a crystal shop on the left hand side of the road. We noticed at the four corners of the building were large rose quartz almost pillar side. We asked the shop owner why she had large rose quartz at the four corners of the building. The owner told us it was for protection and the building had never been disturbed in all the years she had worked there.I couldn't be a metaphysical crystal collector without my large color photo crystal book that explains the properties of the stones and what you can use the stones for. According to the book rose quartz is the stone of love and programs the cells for joy and longevity. Also, it is a powerful healing stone and its frequency is enlightening. You just can't have too much rose quartz in your home. I found a lapidary shop in Golden that sold rose quartz for $2 a pound. There must be about 100 pounds of rose quartz in my apartment now. Rose quartz is in the four corners of my home and in all the windows surrounding the north and west wall which are full of windows. Not only is my home protected from negative energy, my Rolfing office, which is set up in my living room, is full of healing and enlightening energy. Once I set up the rose quartz in my home you could feel the energy shift. The energy felt lighter, softer and very calming.

The crystals and all the clearing we did made a big difference in our health and sense of well being. But we were still getting attacked and having to clear every day, sometimes two or three times a day. We still had no solid answers on how to affect the source that kept plaguing us. We began to notice we were able to change the negative energy and help spirits cross over.

I knew for sure that I needed to keep on my journey for answers and ask the higher powers to guide me in my quest. Speaking of guidance from the higher powers Tim come across an article about energy vampires. The article had pictures of healthy auras that looked like a circle of light around the body, then a contrasting picture of an aura that had been repeatedly attacked by an energy vampire. The circle of light around that attacked body looked dim and you could see holes in the aura. The author of the article explained that, depending on the type of energy vampire, if its prey did not get away from the person who was sucking their life force, the person would become ill. And if the energy vampire persisted to suck the life force from that person eventually the person would die.

The article on energy vampires was just another piece of the puzzle for me. I had felt energy vampires before and if I spent any time around them I would start to feel my energy being drained away. Once I would get away from that said energy vampire I would feel my energy charging back up. But Tim and I were not just dealing with a run of the mill energy vampire. We were dealing with an energy vampire who could drain our life force over the airways. We could not just walk away from this energy vampire. We spent most of our time clearing whoever's life force sucking cords were attaching to us and stealing our life force without our consent or control.

For the last four years of my life I had felt someone or some entity stealing my life force (I was clueless as to what was going on during this time period) and it was taking a toll on my life. I had been sick more than I had ever been in my life and one winter I had bronchitis that included a bad cough for seven months. I had never had bronchitis growing up. Something was happening in my life but I just couldn't put my finger on what was going on. Yet now looking back over the last four years the energy vampire scenario made sense. We had tools to destroy the EV cords that were stealing our life force and then we would start feeling our energy increase. But we weren't able to stop the EV cords from being attached to us again. We spent an enormous amount of time destroying EV cords. We were getting healthy and having more energy. But we needed more answers.

October of 2007 I turned 52 years old. Our health kept improving thanks to all the clearing we did and the 100 or more pounds of crystals we had accumulated in the apartment in the last year. I was hoping to have a better ski year than last year. Thanksgiving rolled around, so Tim and I planned to spend Thanksgiving at Winter Park. We invited my daughter and Tim's nephew. I may have been in better shape for skiing that year but the fall had been warm and there were only two runs of man-made snow to ski on. There's a reason the man-made runs are called ribbons of death. Our one day skiing on ice was not so fun. But the hotel had a great Thanksgiving buffet and that made the two-day ski holiday to Winter Park worthwhile. I would much rather ski for a day than cook all day making Thanksgiving dinner.

Tim and I spent Christmas of 2007 in Boulder and debated whether to buy a real Christmas tree or a faux Christmas tree. My vote was for the real tree, Tim voted for the faux tree. I had my heart set on a real tree and wasn't warming up to a faux tree. Tim was spending Christmas with me, helping me find solutions on how to deal with energy vampires. Since Tim was my guest perhaps I should let him buy the faux tree. I think the higher powers were on Tim's side. A brand new Home Depot was just built in Boulder over the summer. So Tim and I decided to check out the new store. To my amazement Home Depot had the most beautiful faux trees I had ever seen and quite a selection to top it off. The only concession I made to have a faux tree was it would have to look like a real tree. Well, there was the faux tree that looked like a real tree. We bought that beautiful faux tree and set it up in the living room, fired up the pine scented candle and it was almost like having a real Christmas tree.

A fake Christmas tree wasn't the only gift I got for Christmas that year from Tim. I wanted to put a wood burning stove in my fireplace ever since I moved into my apartment. So I shared my desire with Tim. Tim replied let's see what we can find. Off we went looking at all the stores in Boulder that had wood burning stoves. At McGuckin's hardware store, Boulder's favorite hardware store, we found a Jotul wood burning stove that was small enough to fit in my fireplace. Jotul burned so clean that I could burn wood on no burn days. No burn days were usually the coolest days of the year, the days when you needed the extra heat to get the apartment warm and cozy. Jotul had a glass door so I could watch the fire and heat up the living room.

Another thing we learned from the book Mr. Villoldo wrote about spirits is they love fire and are attracted to the flames. Bonus! When we would have a fire going in the woodstove for a few hours all the spirits in the house would be attracted to the flames and bye-bye spirits, up the fireplace and out to the heavens. Some days were worse than others when dealing with the spirit realm or energy vampires. While the wood burning stove was going it seemed to clear the entire apartment of whatever negative energy was brothering us. It seemed like Tuesdays and Saturdays were the worst days of the week for dealing with dark energies. For sure, if we were under attack the woodstove would be burning that day.

That winter I started mentoring a Rolfing student named Beth. I had a feeling that she would be a very talented Rolfer. That was one thing I needed was a talented Rolfer to work on me. I worked with plenty of talented Rolfers in Alaska. If I wanted a Rolfer in Boulder as talented as the Alaska Rolfers I guess I just had to mentor one myself.

Paul Van Alstine came down from Alaska only once a year to trade out a Rolfing session with me. I needed at least one session a month from Paul considering how beat up I was getting from the energy vampire. The reason Paul was able to help dispel the pain in my body from the energy vampire was because Paul worked with the energetic field of the body. That's what energy vampires mess with, the energetic system of the body, and that's what needed to be repaired.

Finally it started snowing in Winter Park and the ski season was good for Tim and me. I was enjoying skiing with Tim. I was happy not to be sick or have pain in my knees or shoulders. What Tim and I were doing to destroy energy vampire cords seemed to be working and our health kept improving.

My daughter came out in March to do some skiing with Tim and me. Thanksgiving Jesse only had two death strips to snowboard on but Winter Park had fresh snow and a lot of it for March. Spring break came with a foot of fresh snow with the whole mountain open. Jesse and I carved plenty of turns and when we're together we share tons of love and laughter.

The first week of April I was doing DL's monthly Rolfing session. How DL managed to get a two hour session from me every month mystified me. After I finished the session and DL had left I would be exhausted for hours after working on DL. It would take me about two or three hours to recover my energy. I thought DL was my friend so I cut DL some slack and didn't schedule any clients on the day I worked on DL. I knew working with DL would take a lot of my energy.

Part Two — Leaving Alaska to Live in Colorado

I just got used to the idea that I would be exhausted after DL's session. That evening I climbed into my comfy bed for a sweet night's sleep. As I lay in bed waiting to fall asleep my legs went numb from my waist to my feet. Freaked out doesn't even begin to describe my fear and panic that I was feeling at that moment. OMG, what is happening to me? I think my guardian angels were trying to calm me down. In my head I heard the words "you need to clear". I was able to get out of my bed, grab my pendulum and start clearing. And to my surprise the feeling came back into my legs. So what I had been doing for months learning to clear and the clearing I did worked that night. Yes!!!!! Still totally mystified I'm wondering, where did that come from? Then my guardian angels showed me a vision while I was still awake of the culprit that had caused my legs to go numb. It was a black cobra with gold stripes running horizontal down its head and back. This black cobra was looking very Egyptian to me.

The next day I shared my experience with Tim. "Gwin," he said, "I don't think DL is your friend at all. I think you're being taken advantage of by DL. I think you need to start thinking that this numbing experience may have come from DL." I told Gil, DL's friend, about my numbing experience and he was just as mystified as I was. I called DL and talked about my experience but DL had no idea where that type of energy could be coming from.

After confronting DL on the phone Tim and I had a falling out. You would think I would be putting 2 + 2 together by now. So I called DL and scheduled a session to help me sort out why Tim and I had a falling out. I told Tim that I had scheduled an appointment to see DL. Tim looked at me and said "Are you serious? You need to cancel that appointment."

At that moment my guardian angels made another intervention. It was like a fog lifted from my brain and the thought in my head was written in neon lights. If you end up going to this session with DL you will be lost to yourself for good. I thought I was in fear when my legs went numb. I knew at that moment I was hearing the truth my guardian angels were desperately making their last intervention. It was the point of no return for me. I was full of anger for being so blind. Fearlessly I left a message on DL's answering machine, at a time I knew no one would be home, and canceled my appointment. Taking up the fight against the dark side I wrote a Dear DL letter explaining that I would no longer be Rolfing DL.

After the Dear DL letter we were getting attacked almost daily. There was no denying the facts now, DL was my worst nightmare. We suffered great pain and energy drain by this shaman, witch, black magic practitioner, and black hole energy vampire. I think it would be safe to say we really pissed DL off. We started calling DL "Dragon Lord", a person who should not be named, for fear of attracting DL's attention.

Tim and I held our own against the daily attacks from DL. We always suffered more on Tuesdays and Saturdays. Perhaps it had to do with the alignment of the planets or someone's schedule, but would we ever know for sure? Tim was running out of money and needed to go back to Alaska for the high dollar jobs. I was very sad to have my friend travel back to Alaska which meant I would be facing DL alone.

Finding Help

I'm blessed with some amazing clients who have been a great resource in my life supporting me in my battle against the dark side. Connie happens to be an extraordinary person, psychologist and my client. Lucky me! I was sharing my story with Connie of my encounter with a healer who was an energy vampire. She shared with me her encounter with a guru who had no boundaries or ethics. Connie had to stay away from that person, couldn't even talk to her on the phone. She also had friends that were having problems with this same guru.

Connie and her friends got together and had a group clearing

Part Two   **Leaving Alaska to Live in Colorado**

to destroy any cords or energy attachment that the guru had formed to steel their life force. They also refused to ever say the guru's name again, see her or talk to her on the phone. So the guru couldn't attach any new psychic energy vampire cords. This stopped the guru from mind control or sucking her clients' energy. It felt good not to be the only person on the planet dealing with this issue. Connie helped me to see that there is light at the end of the tunnel. I just had to explore more avenues.

Tim had left in May for Alaska and I missed his company. It was up to me now to find practitioners that could help me find a way to stop DL from destroying my life.

DL did call me a few weeks after Tim left for Alaska. DL could not understand why I sent the Dear DL letter. DL let me know she didn't like Tim and now that he was gone we could start our Rolfing sessions again. Once again I confronted DL about what happened to me the time my legs went numb. DL tried to tell me it must have come from a client DL had been working with. I told DL I wouldn't be able to Rolf her until I had sorted things out.

I got off the phone and I was in dire pain. I knew I had picked up entities from DL or DL had sent them to cause me pain. I started clearing and the pain would stop, but then start up again. I would clear again and the pain would stop. I knew DL was pissed off at me from the amount of pain I was in. Amazing, I couldn't even talk to DL on the phone without being affected. I knew if I gave in and started working with DL again I would be dealing with more pain than what I was in after our phone conversation.

Summer of 2008 was the lowest point of my life since I had been dealing with DL. I began to wonder if my life was even worth living or if I still wanted to be here on the planet. I had no energy to enjoy my life. At this point in my life I had no idea that my vital energy was at about 30%; that's pretty close to being dead!

I went to Seattle for my annual summer visit with my daughter.

My energy always improved when I left Boulder. Jesse turned me on to Univera. I tried Univera's antioxidant drink and aloe drink and noticed an increase of energy. I liked Univera's very high quality products.

I signed up under Jesse so I could buy Univera at a discount. I ordered Univera's DHEA and it changed the quality of my life. My life made a u-turn as I had enough energy to start enjoying living again. I would discover down the road that I needed to raise my vital energy if I wanted to stay alive and defeat DL.

Thank the higher powers my chiropractor Jon Wall and I had become good friends. We're on the same page when it comes to understanding the power of black magic, shamans, and witches. He was one of the few people that I could talk to and get great advice. We shared many of the same clients and the combination of Rolfing and chiropractic helped speed up the healing process in our shared clients. Jon sent me a client to Rolf who had been training in the psychic arts. Lori talked about her training and things she had learned about protecting herself from dark energies. I told her about DL and what I had been doing to protect myself. Lori wanted to try some of her clearing techniques on me. Lori perceived that DL had two beings living in that body and they were affecting my health.

After finding out from Lori that DL had two beings helping make my life miserable the spider attacks started up again. Since Jon was trying to help guide me in ways to fight DL then he began to get attacked by spiders at his chiropractic office. I'm sure DL planned to make me think that someone else was causing me all this misery. DL wanted me to think she could help me. But DL's true desire was to steal my life force. I've always been a very high energy person until I met DL. I'm sure I was a juicy morsel, giving lots of energy. DL the energy junky wanted her fix of energy, a high quality energy source, and that would be me.

Part Two: Leaving Alaska to Live in Colorado

The Shaman

Jon suggested that I go to the shaman that he had been seeing. I made an appointment with Ken hoping to find some resolution with DL. I met Ken, an African trained shaman, and I liked his energy right away. After our introductions were made, Ken started the session. Ken felt a dark male energy hanging around me from DL. Ken started wondering about the dark energy surrounding me and since DL is an American Indian trained shaman he wanted to consult the Akashic records to see if I had any past Karma with DL. The New Age definition of the Akashic records is a place where all records are kept about every person on the planet by celestial being. Ken started into his vision quest to see what the Akashic records had recorded about any past lives.

Some place in time during the 1700's DL and I belonged in a nature worshipping group. The group used herbs to heal the villagers. The group loved everything about nature, protected the land, and asked for blessings for the land from the higher powers. They were some of the first environmentalists.

One day a man joined this group of nature worshippers. But this was a power hungry man full of dark energy who wanted to use the group's knowledge and energy for his own desires. DL and I had been close friends until this dark man entered the group. Half of the group, including me, refused to join the coven that was forming. The dark man was practicing black magic and DL was drawn completely into this man's power. He promised DL the world with unlimited power and gave his assurance there was no evil involved.

DL was desperate to keep all of the group together and gave us the same promises that the dark man had given DL. The six of us could see that DL was being deceived and lied to. But DL had a lust for life, power, and the tall dark handsome man that temped DL. We went our separate ways, six of the group staying in the light and the other six in the group becoming witches and practitioners of the dark arts. For reasons beyond my comprehension DL thought that I would join again in the present age and become part of the coven. DL must hold some diluted vision of becoming all powerful if we were together or that DL could take my gifts from me. If DL had to destroy me in the process so be it because DL felt entitled and couldn't imagine not getting her way. DL felt that I owed my service. Here is the news, witch, I don't owe you, not in the past, present or future!

The session ended with Ken and all I could think was, "It's always good to know what you're dealing with." One of my favorite sayings is: There are no problems, only solutions. I was going to need a whole lot of solutions to get DL out of my life. Ken told me after the session he didn't feel the dark man's energy around me anymore. I made sure while I was clearing to clear any dark energies that may be trying to steal energy from my aura.

I was impressed with Ken's ability to access the Akashic records and inform me of the past life that was the link between DL and me in this present life of mine. I was not inclined to become a witch or ever be DL's friend. Whoever threw down the gauntlet first I'm not sure but I seemed to be locked in a battle of Light against the Dark whether I wanted it or not. After the session I still had no resolution with DL and I was still suffering pain from DL's attacks. Ken, the shaman, was the second healer to tell me that DL was possessed by two beings. How these beings would affect me I had no clue but I'm sure it couldn't be a good thing. Ken also told me of a psychic snake that had bit him and almost killed him. Ken had gone numb in his upper body and had trouble breathing.

My life with DL wasn't going that good. But my daughter met Eli September 17, 2008 and he would be the love of her life. At the end of October Jesse flew Eli out for an early birthday gift to Colorado to see a Denver Broncos game. Jesse's good friend Marquez (who was playing for the LA Raiders) comped the 3 of us tickets for the football game at Mile High Stadium. Jesse was blown away by how large and tall the stadium was. Jesse said "wow" a lot.

Eli's mother lived only about 10 miles away from me in Arvada,

Part Two   Leaving Alaska to Live in Colorado

and I enjoyed meeting her and Eli's extended family who still lived in the Denver area. Turns out Eli spent his younger years growing up in Colorado. Eli and Jesse's visit lifted my spirits and energy. I liked Eli right away and I was happy to see my daughter well matched.

Jesse and Eli returned home to Seattle and within a few weeks Jesse ended up in the hospital. The emergency room staff thought she might need her appendix taken out. The doctors couldn't find any cause for her symptoms. She couldn't hold down food and what she got down went through her. I had her buy some probiotics and colloidal silver and she did recover after about 3 days. I started clearing Jesse like crazy. I suspected DL of landing my daughter in the hospital. So I made sure from then on I would include my daughter in my daily clearings.

The book that Tim read by Mr. Villoldo talked about a doctor's disbelief in a Peruvian shaman. The shaman told the doctor he would prove his powers. The doctor was heading back to New York and the shaman said he would show the doctor his power on Thursday. Thursday came and went and nothing happened. But come Monday morning the doctor became gravely ill, couldn't keep food down, had diarrhea and his whole body hurt. The doc made a call to his friend in Peru and had him contact the shaman to tell him he believed in his powers and to please stop making him sick. His friend from Peru told him that the shaman was busy and didn't get around to using his power on the doc until Monday. As soon as the shaman got the message the doc's health improved.

Logically it would make sense that if DL were a true shaman DL would be able to send my daughter to the hospital. That would be the reason that the doctors at the hospital couldn't find any cause for her symptoms. The doctors were unable to help her and just sent her home. I think DL's ploy was to make my daughter sick so I would schedule an appointment with DL in hopes that it would help my daughter so DL could start sucking the life force out of me again. DL wants to be thought of as a good person that heals people. DL may be suffering from delusions of grandeur, thinking she can heal people. But the only person getting any help from DL's session is DL. I'm sure DL wouldn't like anyone knowing the truth about who DL really is.

That October my friend Miss Allen and I attended a New Age Halloween party down in Denver. At this particular Halloween party the hostess offered the guests free tarot card readings. I'm a big tarot card fan and never pass up a chance for a reading. I sat down, careful not to give any information away, shuffled the deck of tarot cards and handed them back to our hostess. While you're shuffling the tarot deck you need to be thinking of your question. According to the cards that evening, not only was I up against a talented shaman but also DL was part of a black magic coven. That would mean I was also dealing with a talented witch that had access to that coven's black magic and participants. Tim and I suspected DL of using black magic against us. Another piece of the puzzle confirmed! The hostess suggested that I would need some more help to deal with this person and the coven they belonged to. So, I put it out there to the higher powers that I needed more help.

November I flew to Seattle to spend Thanksgiving with my daughter, get to know Eli better and the three of us would have Thanksgiving dinner with my brother in Port Orchard. Jesse owns a house in Burien and her dream was to remodel her house and turn it into the home of her dreams. Eli just happened to be an architect/contractor, talented and handy around the house. He could do plumbing, wiring, sheet rocking and framing, just the man Jesse needed in her life. Jesse got her wish of remodeling her home, with a lot of work and some inconvenience. When I arrived at Jesse's house there was a 3 foot high pile of sheet rock in the middle of the living room. The pile of sheet rock had come from the wall that used to be between the kitchen and living room. I can't tell you how delighted I was that we were having Thanksgiving dinner at my brother's home, because you couldn't sit down at my daughter's house without getting sheet rock dust all over your clothes. The rest of the holiday Jesse and I went shopping to avoid hanging out in the sheet rock dust.

Part Two   Leaving Alaska to Live in Colorado

Back in Boulder, my son Isaac and I planned to spend Christmas skiing at Vail. I booked 3 nights at Evergreen Lodge in Vail. Last Christmas, the Denver Airport was closed down from blizzards. But what would be the chance that the Seattle Airport would be closed down this Christmas from a huge snowstorm? So sad…Isaac couldn't leave Anchorage because the Seattle Airport was closed. But we decided on a back-up plan. If the Seattle Airport didn't open in time for Christmas we would visit the Grand Canyon in February instead. Since the rooms were nonrefundable, I went ahead and drove to Vail to carve a few turns without Isaac. I checked into the hotel and let the front desk know that my son might make it to Vail for Christmas if the Seattle Airport ever opened. I skied at Vail after I unpacked my belongings and the next day my body hurt so bad I wanted to go home because there was no way that I would be able to ski any more days. I found it very strange that I should hurt so badly after only one day of skiing. I checked out the next day and let the front desk know my son was still stuck in Seattle and I was unable to ski another day. The young ladies at the front desk must have felt really bad for me because they refunded me the two nights that I didn't stay. I just took that as a sign from the higher powers that Isaac and I needed to visit the Grand Canyon. Thank you so much sweet young ladies at the front desk for being so kind.

I skied with Barbara at Vail in January and as much as I love to ski the pain I was dealing with was taking the fun out of it. It hurt my legs just to walk in my ski boots. I would make a few runs in the morning and be exhausted. Then I would wait around at the lodge for Barbara to get done skiing so I could go home. The first two years I skied with Barbara I would wear her out and I would be the one who didn't want to leave the mountain. That was before I met DL and had a few of those wonderful healing session. I now call those sessions smoke and mirrors.

It is so hard for me to believe that I was deceived for so long, four years, and I paid for those sessions in trade with Rolfing. It was destroying my quality of life. By the time DL got done stealing life force from me I had so little life force left I didn't enjoy being alive anymore. Thanks to the higher powers for bringing Tim into my life, my friend who helped me see who DL was and what DL was doing to me. Now that I had broken all ties, DL still stole my life force by being a psychic vampire. I had to clear DL two or more times a day just to keep my energy. I will find a way to stop her for good. I prayed every day to be free from this energy sucking psychic vampire.

Grand Canyon with Isaac

February rolled around and I was looking forward to hanging out with my son and spending some warm days in Arizona. I picked Isaac up at the Denver Airport, he spent the night with me in Boulder and the next day we were back at the airport catching a flight to Phoenix. We spent one night at the Sheraton in Phoenix. That evening we started planning our trip to the Grand Canyon. Early the next morning we headed north toward the Grand Canyon and planned to spend one night in Sedona.

Halfway to Sedona we had to stop at Montezuma Castle National Monument; it was on the way and we couldn't resist. We paid our money at the park entrance, took pictures and played the tourist. I had bought myself a new camera for Christmas that year. My new camera could hold over 2,000 pictures and videos. I hadn't mastered the use of the video option in my camera yet. I love technology and, thanks to my son, I have tech support and have become technology proficient.

Isaac had brought his laptop, camera and two iPods full of music. Isaac and I are both fans of John Mayer. A road trip just isn't a road trip without music. Every time I hear John Mayer's "Gravity" I think of our Arizona road trip. I had brought a book about the energy grids that exist in Sedona. My son began teasing me and asked if I had remembered to bring my hippy book about Sedona. We arrived in Sedona and it was still daylight, plenty of daylight to get great pictures of the rock formations on our drive into town. I was checking in my hippy book, looking at the map for the hikes to the strongest energy grids. But we decided that we should find a

Part Two — Leaving Alaska to Live in Colorado

place to stay because it was getting too late to start on any long hikes shown on the map. After we found a nice hotel we went to search for pizza. Not too far from our restaurant we spied a crystal shop that I just had to check out.

Of course the prices weren't good at this crystal shop and I could have waited for the Gem and Mineral Show in Denver to buy the honey calcite at a lower price, but I had to buy just one piece in Sedona. I found a beautiful light yellow sphere of honey calcite…just the crystal I needed for that trip. Honey calcite is helpful for taking you in a new direction in life. I could use a new direction in my life, so easy to get stuck in a rut. Also honey calcite helps in understanding the divine inspiration and guidance to clear your mind for higher knowledge. I was ready for as much divine guidance as I could get to help me deal with DL. The honey calcite sits on my bookshelf above my computer to inspire divine guidance while I write my story.

We returned to the hotel room, watched a little TV, brushed our teeth and got ready for bed. I was in bed looking at the energy grids on my map trying to pick a hike. Isaac said we didn't even have to go on a hike to feel the energy grids because he could feel the energy grid just lying in bed. I always pride myself on being able to feel the shifts in the energy grids wherever I go. So I tuned my perception to feel what my son was talking about. Oh yes, I could feel the flow of energy below our room. I told my son he was right, the flow of energy under our room was very strong and we didn't even have to go hiking to feel it. I guess I had been feeling the energy flowing ever since we began driving past the rock formations into town. I always feel more energy flow when I'm around my son or daughter. I had to take a moment to perceive the energy flow from the earth. I realized it was boosting both of our energies and being together boosted the energy even more. I was so excited that my son could feel the flow of energy before I even became aware of it. The energy in Sedona is very healing and being with my son is very healing for me. I was starting to feel healthy, have more energy and DL wasn't able to hook into me and steel my energy while in Sedona. My light bulb came on. The higher powers wanted me and my son to travel to Sedona together. It was divine guidance teaching me of the healing powers of the earth and that my son and I shared some of the same psychic gifts! While we were still in Sedona I kept hearing a voice in my head saying that people shouldn't live here. I knew it was a sacred and healing place for the Indians. I wasn't sure if I was hearing the ancestors of the Indians or if the land didn't want people changing the land and disrupting the energy grids of the area. I just kept that insight to myself. Before long my son made the comment, people shouldn't be living here. I know, I have been hearing the same information since we got here. Later I wondered if it wasn't DL messing with us being in Sedona because DL couldn't hook into our life force and steal our energy. Were we totally protected from DL's powers while visiting the area of Sedona?

Morning came with the glow of the warm winter sun and after a yummy waffle breakfast I wanted to drive up to the airport. The airport in Sedona is small and sits on top of a mesa overlooking the town of Sedona. According to the energy grid shown on the map the airport looked like one of the strongest energy grids in the area. We were already so close we might as well see what we could discover.

My son was a little skeptical about the drive to the airport but once we arrived at the top of the mesa the view was breathtaking. We knew we had started our morning at the right place. My new camera got a workout that morning. We had a 360 degree view of the surrounding area and all the rock formations. It was like having a virtual map of the area. Then we found a hike with a view of the valley we had driven up the day before for another round of picture taking. The large sandstone formation where we stood was very energizing. We could have stayed there for hours just soaking up the view and the energy we felt. I felt peaceful and comforted by the earth. But we only had a five day vacation and we had planned a hike on Devils Bridge before driving to the Grand Canyon that day. It was hard to leave the tranquil setting of the Airport Mesa but we had a lot of ground to cover today.

Part Two — Leaving Alaska to Live in Colorado

Next we had a two mile hike to Devils Bridge, a large rock arch that you can hike on. The scenery on the hike was beautiful like all of Sedona, with great energy. We had fun exploring the trails and rock formations on the way to Devils Bridge. Once we arrived at the arch I took one look at the shear drop off and I couldn't go any further. I have a fear of heights next to shear drop offs and suffered an attack of vertigo. My son hiked out on the arch for me to take his picture but there was no way that I would be able to walk out on that arch. I did get a good picture of Isaac standing on the Devils Bridge Arch. We took pictures to show evidence of our adventure so we could move on to our next tourist attraction.

The next stop on our speedy tourist tour of Arizona was Slide Rock State Park. My son brought his swimming trunks, the day was sunny, but there was some snow still left on the ground from the last week's snowstorm. The river ran through a formation of red rocks and the summer would be a great time to slide down through the red rocks and cool off. The more time we spent taking pictures of the river the less inclined Isaac was to put on his swim trunks for the ride down the river through the red rocks.

I kept noticing the healing energy from the red rocks and the surrounding land formation that were left from years of the river cutting a pathway into the layers of earth. I kept feeling better having more energy and it felt great to have enough energy to enjoy my life, be with my son and experience the beauty of this land.

As we continued on our drive we were gaining elevation and climbing out of the canyon into forests deep with snow. Isaac's friend said that at the top of the canyon we would find the best place to buy Indian jewelry. We arrived to find the Indian market starting to close down but still in time for me to buy a silver and lapis bracelet. Lapis is a powerful protective stone against physical danger and psychic attacks. Lapis combined with silver enhances the power of the lapis. Silver draws negativity from the body and transfers positive energy of the mineral into the body's aura. It cleans the body via the pores and eliminates toxins at the cellular level. Silver also acts as an anti-bacterial and anti-viral agent. Just the kind of jewelry I needed for protection from a certain dark shaman.

Once you get to Flagstaff you have two directions to choose from to reach the Grand Canyon, Route 180 or 89. We chose Route 180 that skirts a small mountain. Flagstaff had about 2 feet of snow during our drive by and Route 180 ended up being the snowy route. The closer our drive brought us to the Grand Canyon we noticed the snow levels declining. We were definitely pushing our time line for the day but we were able to find the Grand Canyon and catch a fading glimpse at sunset of the canyon. My first impression of the Grand Canyon was breathtaking and I understood why they named the canyon Grand. We could see the canyon at sunset but the pictures we took looked like we were just taking pictures at night, no distinguishing details. Our arrival at the Grand Canyon was followed by dropping temperatures and as our higher power guides would have it the cold front encouraged a drop in the room rates. We could afford to book a room overlooking the Grand Canyon.

My son and I enjoy staying up late at night; we're not really morning people. Our plan was to get up for the sunrise and shoot some spectacular pictures. We checked into our room and I took a shower knowing I wouldn't have time in the morning to take a long hot shower. It was Thursday night and we watched *Lost*; it was the 5th season and I didn't want to miss an episode. That night I couldn't get warm and didn't get much sleep either. In the morning my son noticed I had my coat on top of the covers on top of me. He asked if I was cold and I reply Yes! "Mom, I was nice and warm all night; my bed was by the heater." I had picked the wrong bed.

Come morning it was 16 degrees outside. So I put on two shirts, my fleece vest, coat and two pairs of pants. All that my son brought was a fleece jacket. Being from Alaska he thought he would be warm enough. We drove out on the West Rim Drive, found a place to park, and walked out to the rim of the Grand Canyon. With our cameras in hand we got into position to catch the sun peek above the walls of the canyon. It was cold but we did get some great pictures.

Part Two   Leaving Alaska to Live in Colorado

What I realized was we would have gotten spectacular pictures at sunset rather than morning. Sharing the sunrise in the morning seemed to energize the day even though we were both freezing.

We were both ready for breakfast after god knows how many calories we burned that morning trying to keep warm while taking pictures of the sunrise peeking over the canyon. Oh! How I love hot chocolate to warm up with in the morning while I'm waiting for my food to arrive. Our plan for the day was to hike to the bottom of the canyon, but the week before a winter storm had dumped about 3 feet of snow on the entire trail and down into the canyon.

The mules weren't taking any riders down into the canyon because of the slick conditions. I told my son as much as I would love to hike to the river at the bottom of the canyon I would sure hate to slide off one of the canyon tails and plummet to my death or even worse hurt myself and survive. Isaac was disappointed but we agreed to come back another time to hike when the trails would be dry.

After breakfast we loaded up the Dodge Charger, the muscle car that my son rented that he had to have for our road trip. I was totally into having a hot looking muscle car to cruise around in. The blue Charger was one of my favorite car colors. If you have ever seen the 70's movie *Vanishing Point* the Dodge Charger would be the ultimate cruising car. The day was beautifully sunny with clear blue skies and was warming up. Isaac drove the East Rim Drive of the canyon and along the way we would stop to take pictures at every pull off along with everyone else that wanted to visit the Grand Canyon in the winter. The pictures we took were spectacular and the vistas were a treat for the eyes and thrilling for the senses.

Our next destination was the Watchtower on the edge of the Grand Canyon with an even more enticing view of the Grand Canyon. While driving to our next destination we began talking about the energy we were feeling from the canyon Isaac felt that the energy was stronger at the Grand Canyon than in Sedona. I couldn't tell the difference between the two areas. I've noticed while staying at

Moab when I first arrive I can feel the energy strongly. But after 2 or 3 days I don't feel the energy as much. I think what happens is my body adjusts to the healing frequency of the area. My cells start vibrating at the frequency of the earth, which is a strong healing frequency according to New Age philosophy.

As the frequency of my body changed to match that of the canyon, I didn't feel the energy difference because my cellular energy began to match the area where I'm staying. The first night I spent next to the canyon I was freezing and didn't get a good night's rest. I was too distracted to check into the earth's energy that evening and compare it to Sedona. Even though we were up early we had plenty of energy while stopping along the canyon's rim taking pictures. It would make sense to feel more energy next to the Canyon rather than Sedona. The sheer size of the Grand Canyon would cause us to have more exposure to the energy of the earth's core.

The drive from Grand Canyon Village along the rim of the canyon to the Watchtower is 25 miles providing an amazing perspective of the expansiveness of the canyon.

The Watchtower is a round building constructed of natural rock from the area with a circular staircase ascending along the inside of the outer wall up 4 flights of stairs. The walls are painted with Indian designs. The energy felt very sacred, a place that the Indians would hold in high regard. Being in the Watchtower gave me the sense of soaring over the canyon and having a bird's eye view. I could feel the grandeur of the canyon, a sense of being part of the whole. Any emptiness that I may have felt in my being was filled up with a peaceful awe of beauty.

After the visit to the top of the Watchtower I was ready to leave since we were unable to hike to the bottom of the canyon. Isaac and I agreed that we didn't want to back track 25 miles to Grand Canyon Village. Isaac was concerned that perhaps I wasn't ready to leave because the goal of this vacation was to see the Grand Canyon. We must have the same attention span. But I'm sure that we're both

Part Two — Leaving Alaska to Live in Colorado

a little sad to leave the grandeur and energy of the Grand Canyon that made us both feel such well being. Our time was limited and the next day we would be catching our flight to Denver. Heading back to Flagstaff our adventure would take us on the eastern Route 89.

The eastern route is dry, more desert-like, warmer and no snow. I like this route much better and it seems a shorter route to Flagstaff. On this route we found plenty of places to stop and buy Indian jewelry. We stopped at a few of the pull offs and I bought a turquoise and silver necklace. Turquoise is healing and cleansing of pollutants. The stone is protective, helps with clarity, purifying energy, helps with absorption of nutrients and regeneration of tissue. It is a stone for finding wholeness, truth and wisdom. I'm all for buying any stone that is protective.

By the time we hit Flagstaff we both were grumpy. I thought all we needed was some lunch because we just traveled 82 miles across a desolate desert. Lunch did seem to take the edge off our bad moods. Perhaps the loss of the feeling of well being that we felt at the rim of the Grand Canyon was affecting our bad mood.

After lunch I set my sights on spending a warm night in Phoenix. We had almost a full day before we caught our flight back to Denver and my thoughts turned to soaking up the warm sun on our last day of vacation. We checked into the Sheraton for the evening after driving all day from the Grand Canyon. All I could think about was a warm comfortable bed for the evening. I was so looking forward to catching up on my sleep tonight. According to my son I did get a good night's sleep but it was a while before Isaac got to sleep. The next morning Isaac asked if I had heard all the noise outside of our room last night. NO! What happened? Five minutes after you fell asleep a domestic argument arose right outside of our room. The police were called to break up the fight. They had an altercation with the couple and had to take them to jail for disturbing the peace. "Really?" I said, "I didn't hear a sound after I feel asleep. When did you get to sleep?" Isaac said, "About two hours after you got to asleep."

Psychic Gifts in the Modern World

Both my son and I love cars so we went to the Toyota dealer in Phoenix to test drive cars. I was ready to replace my Mustang. I was looking for an AWD vehicle that would get 30 miles to the gallon and if I could find it I would buy it. But my dream car had to look good too. We weren't on the lot very long before a row of cars caught my attention. Toyota Matrix was the car that caught my eye and I let Isaac test drive the car for his insight. I'm not sure the salesman at the Toyota dealer appreciated the way my son test drove the Matrix.

I was pretty sure that after that test drive I would trade my Mustang in on a new Matrix. My son's dream job would be to own a car lot because he loves everything about cars and trucks. He is always buying and selling cars one at a time. Isaac has spent plenty of time test driving cars and trucks. He definitely has the skinny on how much a car is worth and which car has the best performance.

We enjoyed our last sunny warm day in Phoenix but had to return the Charger to the rental car lot and catch our flight back to Denver. Isaac had one day with me in Boulder before he returned to Alaska. We thought about looking at cars but we both decided to enjoy the day in Boulder and rest up. The five vacation days we spent in Arizona were nonstop. Most of those hours were spent in the car. I was burned out on being in a car so we went for a hike for our last day together that overlooked Boulder. It felt good to get some exercise and not have to jump back into a car. I was very sad to see my son leave. What an amazing road trip we shared. I'm sure I have at least 400 pictures to validate the fun we had!

Vacation over; back to reality, except on Thursdays I skied with Barb. I traded in my Mustang for the Matrix AWD that got 30 mpg on the highway. Barb liked my new car. She thought it was cute. It handled way better than the Mustang and I felt much safer in the Matrix. I was totally surprised when Barb and I started skiing. I felt a big energy shift and my skiing was enjoyable and I wasn't in pain.

Part Two — Leaving Alaska to Live in Colorado

I knew that the trip my son and I had taken to Sedona and the Grand Canyon was very healing for me. The heavy energy drain I was experiencing before the trip while skiing had been significantly reduced since my return to Vail Mountain. The trip to Arizona was like getting my battery recharged. I had to find some way to keep my energy up or find a way to keep a certain someone from draining my energy. I wasn't back to my 100% amazing ski self yet but my health and energy were moving to the positive end of the scale. A few facts I'm sure of is being around family helps raise my energy. Being away from Boulder stops me from losing energy. When I first moved to Boulder I could feel the energy from the land and I felt very energized living in Boulder, until I started working with DL. Then my energy began to fall off along with my health and my ability to enjoy life.

In April I spent a 3 day weekend in Seattle with my daughter and her boyfriend Eli. Once again I noticed when I left Boulder the energy drain that I always experienced would stop. The time I would spend with my daughter would charge me back up. I didn't want to move away from Boulder. I worked hard to start a Rolfing practice there. For now all I could do was stick to my daily regimen of clearing DL's life force sucking energies. I always feel my energy come back up after I clear. It's an everyday battle just to hold on to my energy. Some days my body is filled with pain. But after clearing for an hour or so and calling on the higher powers to help me the pain leaves. I pray nightly for guidance to help me find a way to battle the darkness.

Turning Point

May marked another turning point regarding my battle to regain my health and life back. Beth, the student I had been mentoring while she was training at the Rolf Institute, had finished her training and was officially a full-fledged certified Rolfer. Beth was one of most talented students I have mentored for Rolfing. When I received a Rolfing session from Beth, she could integrate my structure and when the body is integrated properly the body's energy increases. It's an energy that the Rolfer and client can both feel when it happens.

Psychic Gifts in the Modern World

I had to let Bridge go, the Rolfer I had been exchanging work with for a few years because when I received a session from Bridge my energy would stay the same, and most times after a session with him I needed to see my chiropractor after my Rolfing session. I had a suspicion DL was able to suck my life force through Bridge while he was Rolfing me, and most likely was also stealing Bridge's life force.

Since Raymon's class, I had started clearing my clients. There would be times when I would pick up an entity, being or spirit, and I would find myself becoming tired. Once I cleared the energies I picked up from a client I wouldn't be tired anymore. I would feel the shift in my energy as soon as I cleared. Beth has that energetic gift and is able to feel her energy shift when she picks up life draining energies from a client and can clear herself from those draining energies. Beth can also see auras change and feel the energy increase when she works on her clients. Since Beth and I understand the energy piece of bodywork we are able to block DL from stealing our energy while we trade out Rolfing work. The Rolfing work is once again recharging my battery like it did before DL started interfering in my life. I knew that Beth was a blessing and that the higher powers were answering my pleas for help.

Paul Miller had been a client of mine for about 9 months and I had gotten to know him well over the course of time. Paul is an electrical contractor and also an amazing healer and teacher. I told him my story of DL and he told me his story of the kind of healing work he does. I was impressed and became interested in trading some sessions with Paul.

Paul came along in my life just in the nick of time. We started trading work June of 2009. I was at the point in my life where I was starting to wonder if what I was experiencing in my life was real. But the first session with Paul was very supportive of my sanity. Paul confirmed what I had been hearing from other psychics, that DL had two beings that were helping to disrupt my life for the past 6 years.

Part Two — Leaving Alaska to Live in Colorado

Resentment? I have huge amounts of resentment. Six years, seriously, that anyone would do that to another person. That is just beyond my ability to understand that kind of self-centeredness and evil. It was good to hear Paul say that DL was the darkest person (black as coal) he had ever dealt with. Not good for me that I was dealing with such a dark person. But it was helpful for me to understand that it would take such as dark person to cause me such misery.

At my first session with Paul, he had to psychically pull DL away from me so he could repair all the holes DL had put in my aura. DL, and beings, had been stealing my life force, which had been causing holes in my aura, in turn causing me to lose energy. My analogy: It's like poking a straw in the drink box and drinking all the juice out. Image all these cords emanating from DL and the evil beings that would suck my life force 24/7. At my lowest point when I wasn't sure whether I would survive or not, I was thinking that it was Dragon Boy causing me to be ill which wasn't the case at all. DL and the beings didn't want to give up their juicy drink box. They didn't want me to realize who was making me ill. They just used Dragon Boy to confuse me and keep me from seeing the truth as long as possible. That's why DL hated Tim Saunders so much, because he exposed the truth to me, that DL was using me. Totally lied to my face, pretending to be my friend.

After a few sessions with Paul he was amazed that DL was back. Tell me about it, I've been clearing this witch for years and DL would not leave me alone. DL reminds me of a big mean dog and there is no way in heaven and on earth that dog is going to let go of a juicy bone.

I have always been a very high energy person and I have true psychic gifts. For DL, my energy was like crack, except the side effects were reversed. As my life force was stolen and my aura destroyed, I fell extremely ill. DL's health had been on the decline for years and its healing powers were non-existent. The one thing DL is really good at is being a psychic vampire. If a healer ever asks you if they can psychically call on you to use your energy for healing, that is a big NO, N-O. If a healer has to use other people's powers for healing they are not a true healer. You are a true healer only if you call on the higher powers to heal.

The energy from the higher powers is infinite and you would never need your client's energy. If you were to agree to give your energy to a healer, the healer now has unlimited access to your life force and you agreed to it. DL asked me if it was alright to psychically call on me to help people. DL wasn't using my energy to heal people. DL can't survive without the client's energy. For reasons unknown to me DL is unable to hook up to the higher powers for energy. Paul had to help me break the contract I had made with DL by agreeing to let DL psychically use my energy. I was clueless to what I had agreed to and how it would affect my life.

Of course DL isn't going to tell me about sucking the life force out of my body and ruining my health. Who would agree to that? DL just smiled at me, told me she loved me and created more holes in my aura so as to suck more of my life force. When I confronted DL about the health problems DL said, "It wasn't me. It must have been someone else." My kids at 10 years old could tell better lies than that.

Now that Paul had a greater understanding of what he was dealing with he would just have to psychically call for more help from the higher powers. During another one of Paul's healing sessions he used his mind's eye to see what other damage DL had caused. When Paul took a look at my bones he said they were full of blackness. He said that DL was like a disease eating away my bones. With his mind's eye Paul started pulling the blackness out of my bones (giving the blackness to the higher powers) and asked me to imagine my bones turning pink. I had to replace the blackness in my bones with healing pink energy. After Paul pulled the black energy from DL out of my bones I began to feel like my old self (before DL) and I had more energy.

Part Three — Fighting the Dark Side

Part Three

Fighting the Dark Side

Part Three — Fighting the Dark Side

Powerful Champion

After another amazing session with Paul I felt my energy double. Paul was the first healer who actually had the tools to go into battle with DL and heal my body from all the damage and illness that DL had caused. It's not an easy battle fighting a powerful shaman, especially one that has no boundaries or ethics. I started having more clarity in my mind and more energy for my clients. I took the tarot card reader's advice to heart and found some help. It was no accident that Paul Miller entered my life by becoming one of my clients. The higher powers were at work in my life giving me a healer to help me battle the blackness that DL haunted me with. I'm sorry to say, but Paul's wife became ill because Paul was helping me. Then Paul had to clear his wife of DL's energy. DL highly disapproved of me working with Paul and lashed out at Paul and his loved ones. With Paul's help DL's energy supply from me was cut off. Addicts, especially psychic vampires, become extremely pissed off when their energy supply is cut off.

DL was extremely angry with Paul's champion healing efforts on my behalf and we both were on her bad side. Even if you didn't fight DL you would still be on DL's bad side. DL started to lash out at our families and our jobs. DL would always attack me on the days I worked with Paul and made me feel bad or Paul would get psychically attacked and his body would hurt more. I would have to clear DL so there wouldn't be any interference with our session. The more health I gained from my sessions with Paul the stronger my aura and I became. The more strength I gained the harder it became for DL to steal my energy.

In July of 2009, my son Isaac was sick for a week with the same symptoms my daughter had the year before that landed her in the hospital. My son ended up in the hospital in Anchorage after his trip to Chicago. Isaac was sick a week in Chicago before he even arrived home. The doctors couldn't find a thing wrong with my son and released him from the hospital. He was sick for another week and none of the alternative remedies that I suggested helped him. We have a good friend of the family who is a PA. I advised Isaac to see Pat and get some antibiotics. My son didn't want to bother Pat (Pat loves Isaac like a son). "Isaac", I replied, "Pat will be more upset with you if she finds out you are sick and you didn't ask her for help." After three weeks of being sick, Isaac finally started getting better when he began taking the antibiotics.

I was pretty upset that witch DL would go after my children. What did DL think would be accomplished from attacking my children? Did DL think I would rush madly to her house and beg her to take my life force and leave my children alone? Not! Never mess with a mother's children, especially if you don't want to piss a mother off. That only encouraged Paul and me to fight harder against DL and work to find ways to protect our family from DL's dark energies.

I'm a person that's pretty easily entertained. That distracts me from my alternative life of dealing with the dark side. Some days I actually have a normal life. I love going to the new Apple Store in Boulder and playing with the iPhones. Even if you don't plan on buying an iPhone, you know that you're only playing with fire when you hang out at the Apple Store. One day I woke up and I had to have an iPhone and that I better buy my daughter one too. My daughter is so hard to buy for and I knew she would love to have an iPhone. It could be her birthday and Christmas present. Even though it would cost me to break my contract with Verizon, I decided I couldn't live without an iPhone and it was so easy for me to justify the purchase of two iPhones. Jesse had been dropping hints for months saying she would love to have an iPhone and was ecstatic that I offered to gift her with one.

Just the previous month my son had purchased an iPhone. If my son had an iPhone why couldn't I have one? I had another great reason to buy iPhones. My son could call Jesse and me and it would make it affordable for Isaac to keep in touch. For the first time ever we would be on the same phone service. It definitely is my responsibility to help my small family keep in touch with each other. I'm happy to say, I love my iPhone and it should be listed as the 8th wonder of the world.

September is always a great month to be in Boulder because the weather is perfect. Another year rolled by and it was time again for the Gem and Mineral Show in Denver. It's like Christmas for me in September. Yes! Beth, my official Rolfer now, wanted to check out the Gem and Mineral Show with me. Beth brought her mother Jenny who had a resale number so we could enter the resale side of the Gem and Mineral Show. I was so excited as it would be the first time that I had been able to see the resale side of the Gem and Mineral Show. It was the girls' weekend out. The reason Beth wanted to buy crystals was because she could tell the difference when she worked on me at my office because of all the crystals under my Rolfing table verses when she worked at her home without crystals under her Rolfing table. I agreed with Beth and told her it's because the client has more energy from the crystals to make changes in their structure. Beth was up for all the energy she could put under her Rolfing table to help her client's change.

There are so many beautiful crystals full of healing energy, where to begin? So many crystals to buy yet being on a budget I have had to devise some strategies for buying crystals before I reach the end of my budget. I leave my credit cards at home, only bring cash and I do allow myself to bring one debit card, just in case I find a crystal whose price is too good to pass up or it's a piece I've been looking for a few years. The most important crystals are the ones I put under my table. I have to buy them first. The three major healing crystals I put under my Rolfing table are quartz, rose quartz and amethyst. Then the pretty decorative crystal I buy next. On the last day of the show the girls and I spent the day buying crystal beads to make jewelry. I wear different crystals for different purposes. For example, I wear pink tourmaline to repair holes in my aura. Pink tourmaline is known for its loving and healing energies. Pink tourmaline has high amounts of lithium and is a very calming stone. I wear a necklace of black tourmaline for psychic protection from DL. Black tourmaline also protects my energy field against attachments, entities, clears negativity, disharmony and cleanses my auric field.

This year at the G & M Show I found a large amethyst piece about 2 feet tall to go next to my fireplace for a great price. I had been looking 3 years for an amethyst that worked within my budget. I wanted to buy a larger piece but realized I would be the one who had to carry the amethyst formation up the stairs and into my apartment. My newly acquired amethyst weighed 43 pounds according to my bathroom scale. I struggled to carry it from the car, up the stairs and into my apartment, and I was very grateful I didn't buy the larger one. I decided the one I bought was just perfect.

 I bought three new crystals and placed them in my living room where I Rolf clients. It takes me a while to get the placement just right in the room when I bring new crystals home. Except for the amethyst on the fireplace I had already decided the perfect placement for my new amethyst. Once I placed my citrine tower and new lapis sphere, I sat down in the middle of the living room seeing if I could feel any changes in the energy of the room. The room was definitely amped up. I was wondering if I would be able to handle the new energy that filled the room from these new crystals. After a week I had an answer to my question. The cells of my body changed frequency to match that of the abundant energy emanation from my new crystals. The room didn't feel like it was full of more energy than I could handle. Even though the room felt back to normal it was my body frequency that had changed to match the energy of the room. I noticed that my Rolfing changed my client's tissue quicker with less work.

I failed to mention the giant crystals that are for sale in the resale building of the Gem and Mineral Show...two to five foot tall quartz towers or quartz spheres a foot in diameter! Prices for these crystals run from $2,000 to $10,000, and matching 6 foot tall amethyst formations run $8,000!

When you stand in front of an assortment of 40 giant crystals the energy flow from these crystals is so overwhelming you can't stand there very long even though it feels very energizing. Beth and her mom enjoyed standing in front of the beautiful giant crystals but also became overwhelmed with the massive amounts of energy produced by so many giant crystals.

My living room office is only a small reproduction of the energy we felt at the Gem and Mineral Show. But the crystals I do have in my living room are powerful healers. I know that the crystals provide healing energy for my clients. I can feel the difference in my body and know the crystals provide energy for my cells to heal. Beth noticed a shift in the energy of my Rolfing office from my new crystals. Before starting her Rolfing session, Beth could feel more energy in the room. Having the crystals in my home has given me another way to raise my energy level so my body can heal and provide protection against DL.

I was still Rolfing Gil who was still good friends with DL but I had learned not to tell Gil anything that I didn't want DL to know. I was sure Gil thought nothing of telling DL what was going on in my life. I shared with Gil that I had bought a new iPhone and just loved it. I didn't think anything about it when my iPhone started having problems. Within a month of Rolfing Gil my iPhone wouldn't work at all. This was my brand new shiny iPhone I had only for 2 months. I had to take my iPhone to the Apple doctor. The

Apple technicians were able to revive my iPhone. My iPhone was working but it still would lock up once in a while. I called home tech support, my son, and Isaac told me what buttons to push on my iPhone to get it working again.

One of the many bits of information that Tim and I learned from Raymon Grace's pendulum class is phones and computers have crystals in them and can be infected by entities or can pick up dark energies. When an electronic device like my iPhone picks up an entity or dark energy, these energies can interfere with the proper functioning of the device. I had been clearing my computer and the last time DL called me on my home phone I cleared my home phone. So I started clearing my iPhone and noticed that it worked better.

My 54th Birthday

Jesse flew to Denver so we could celebrate my 54th birthday together. I love Glenwood Springs and wanted to share this beautiful, magical place with Jesse.

I remember back in July my brother Paul and his family flew in from Seattle and spent a week with me in Colorado. I persuaded my brother to spend 3 days in Glenwood Springs so I went ahead and booked us two hotel rooms at the America Inn. The great thing about staying in Glenwood Springs is you park your car and you can walk everywhere. Our first day we checked out the Hotel Colorado. In the basement of Hotel Colorado is Canyon Bikes where my brother rented bikes for the family.

I have heard rumors that the Hotel Colorado is haunted. I totally agree with the rumors because I could just feel the ghosts or spirits, whether they had chosen to stay or were trapped, afraid to cross over and were staring out of the windows at me. I was very happy that we had chosen to stay at a brand new hotel in Glenwood. I was on vacation and didn't feel like dealing with any apparitions.

Part Three — Fighting the Dark Side

For years I wanted to ride the 16 mile bike trail along the river. On our second day at Glenwood Springs we caught a shuttle to the top of Glenwood Canyon and biked downhill along the Colorado River. The bike trail is one of the most beautiful scenic rides along the Colorado River that I have had the pleasure of riding. My sister-in-law Karen thought we would be biking on some dirt road out in the middle of nowhere. The trail is paved along the river and there are four rest stops along the way with nice restrooms and drinking fountains. If you are inclined you can buy a soda from one of the pop machines. Karen was very relieved that we weren't too far from civilization. I assured her I would never take her and the family out into the middle of the wilderness for a bike trip.

As you are riding along the Colorado River you can watch the whitewater rafters float down the river. In the calm water the rafts floating down the river looked very peaceful. I noticed that Paul kept eyeing the rafters float by when we would take our rest breaks. By the summer I had learned how to use the video feature on my new camera. I took plenty of Colorado River videos to watch on my computer to keep summer alive over the winter months. Paul and Megan, his youngest daughter, were in a race for the finish of the bike ride. They stopped for a short break to watch the rafters pull over in the calm water and jump off the rafts for a swim to cool off from the hot day.

By the time all of us had reached the end of our bike ride Paul and Megan were hot to sign up for a raft trip for the third day of our stay in Glenwood. How convenient that we could sign up for a raft trip at the same place Paul had rented his bikes for the canyon bike ride. Karen and I weren't too excited about turning over while rafting the Colorado River. But Paul, Megan and Nicole had the winning votes so tomorrow, no matter how reluctant Karen and I were for a swim in the Colorado River, we signed our names to the consent forms. Karen had a long talk with the rafting company we were taking our journey down the river with and in 27 years they had only had two rafts turn over in the river. That sounded like pretty good odds to Karen, which gave me a good sense of surviving our raft trip. At least I would be with my family if anything did happen. So much for positive thinking on my part. It's a little harder to practice what you preach when you're maybe facing your last day.

My brother had never whitewater rafted in his life and it was one of the things on his wish list he wanted to do before he died. A large group met at the Hotel Colorado in the morning to go over safety precautions, like how tight to wear your life vest so it worked properly to save your life; where to grab the life vest if one of your companions fell off the raft, and once you grab the life vest how to pull your raft mate back into the raft; and then if you were to fall into the whitewater how to float properly down the river to keep from breaking your legs. After going over the safety regulations I felt rather confident about my chances of surviving. Not!

I made it to the drop off place for the rafts with the family because I couldn't think of a way to sneak off the bus. Lucky us, we got our own raft together. We numbered 5 in our family group and six all together counting the raft handler, a lovely young lady. As we were sitting in the raft waiting to pull out on the river, our lovely guide began giving us instructions on when and how to paddle the raft in the river. Nothing like on the job training. If she can make it down the river so could I.

At the safety precaution meeting in the morning we all met the photographer who would be taking our pictures as we're crashing through the whitewater waves. The photographer rode his bike down the bike path that we rode down the day before. He could bike faster than the rafts could go down the river. Our guide pointed out where we could give a big smile to the photographer as we paddled our raft down the raging rapids. My goal was to try and keep my eyes open so I didn't miss my one and only raft trip. I lived in Colorado for eight years and had never ventured out on the Colorado River, or for that matter any river. I can't really count the canoe trip I took on the Swanson River in Alaska. The river was more like a stream that was deep enough to float a canoe on and at no time was there a chance of being swept downstream. The Swanson River meandered at a slow pace and the water was waist deep at its deepest point.

We launched our raft into the river and by the time we hit the white water my toes where firmly wedged in the seam of the raft and I was paddling for my life. By the time we entered our last set of rapids I was having a great time. To my surprise by the time we finished floating the rapids I was ready to do it again. The last section of the river became a calm, peaceful float. As we floated past Glenwood Hot Springs our guide showed us where the water from GHS dumps back into the river. Our guide also showed us other hot springs along the river that dumped into the Colorado. We reached shore, pulled the raft out of the water and headed back to Hotel Colorado. After changing into dry clothing the pictures of our rafting adventure were ready to view.

It's amazing what action shots the photographer caught with his camera. In one picture the raft and its occupants looked engulfed by the river. As we started into the first set of rapids the pictures showed a serious look on my face, a look that was covering up my fear. By the last set of rapids I had the biggest of smiles on my face. The photos of our summer rafting adventure made a great Christmas photo.

Soaking in Glenwood Hot Springs felt wonderful after our rafting trip. The hot springs are very healing. The hot water has a multitude of trace minerals that the human body can soak up through the skin. The body takes whatever trace minerals it needs from the water. Trace minerals are the building blocks of our bones and tissue. Paul commented on how good the hot springs were making his body feel. I replied to Paul that was why when any relatives come into town I loved sharing Glenwood Hot Springs with them.

So when Jesse asked me what I wanted to do for my 54th birthday I said let's take a road trip to Glenwood Springs. We drove down to Glenwood in October and the canyon is not as spectacular in fall but still breathtaking. The drive is 176 miles from Boulder and worth the drive if you have family to share the scenery with.

Glenwood Springs has one of the largest hot springs pools in the world and one of my favorite hot springs in Colorado. Upon our arrival in Glenwood we headed straight for the pool. With a quick change into our suits and a cool dash to the hottest pool we took our ease in the hot water. The hot water felt so fabulous after being in the car for 3 hours. Jesse noticed her lungs and sinuses were soothed by the hot springs. I could also breathe easier and felt my muscles relax. I like swimming in the larger pool that's cooler but still warm. Jesse just stayed in the hot pool to heal her lungs and sinuses. After 2 hours of soaking, we were starving. Since it was my birthday I chose the restaurant. I'm not sure which I love more, the Mexican food or the margaritas. Glenwood has a great Mexican food restaurant called Margarita's and my brother and his family would agree with me. Jesse and I had a great dinner with a great margarita. Without any warning I was wearing a fancy sombrero and hearing the birthday song in Spanish. "Good one Jesse," I said. I had a wonderful birthday because Jesse was in Glenwood Springs to celebrate with me turning 54. The hot springs, I found out, are another great way for me to raise my energy level.

Reasons to Buy a Computer

My computer was about 6 years old and slow as cold honey. My son and daughter were always complaining about how slow my computer was. I had been surfing on line and pricing HP touch screen computers. My iPhone has spoiled me and I keep touching the screen of my old computer and nothing happens. I was in Best Buy in Boulder buying some ink for my printer. I was wondering to myself if Best Buy had any touch screen computers.

The last time I was in Best Buy there were no touch screen computers. Since I was already there it wouldn't hurt to check. Best Buy had the computer I had been looking for and it was on sale. I called Isaac and asked him if the touch screen was a good price. Most of the time when I call my son he tells me I could have found it for less. But this time Isaac said it was a good deal, buy it. I was so proud of myself that I found a good deal and I bought myself a new HP touch screen. It's the middle of November and I hadn't planned on buying a new computer yet, but hey, it would make a great early Christmas present to myself. I could actually touch the screen and something would happen. The HP computer was the perfect complement to my iPhone. This HP was the highest quality computer I had ever bought, at the lowest price and included Windows 7.

Paul, my healer, said I needed to write the book. The book? Nine years earlier during my last summer in Alaska, Jewel, a channeler from Crestone, Colorado, told me I would be writing a book. I just laughed at the notion of me writing anything. I was a story teller, not a writer. Over the years living in Boulder I had my tarot cards read at least once or twice a year. Two different tarot cards readings that I had paid good money for alleged I needed to write a book. I asked Paul if I had to write the book. After Paul told me I had to write the book, I finally gave in and decided I better write the book since my spirit guides had been trying to tell me for years I would be writing a book. I just didn't want to believe them. If I had to write a book, of course I needed a new computer.

Road Trip

I took two weeks off in December to drive my new Matrix to Seattle for Christmas. Two years in a row my Christmas plans had been foiled by snow closing airports. I didn't want to take any chances not making it to Seattle for Christmas. But it did take me 3 days to drive from Boulder. I liked having my own car in Seattle so I could drive to visit my dad and brother.

I was so happy to see that Jesse and Eli had finished the remodel on the living room and kitchen. I didn't have to worry about sitting in sheet rock dust; that was a good thing. Eli and Jesse did a beautiful job remodeling the living room and kitchen. The remodel made the house look classic and expensive. It only took hours of slave labor and quite a few of Eli and Jesse's weekends that saved them the high cost of a remodel. I had my own bedroom and bathroom.

My accommodation was as good as any 4 star hotel in Seattle.

I started telling Jesse she had the perfect man (which I have always been a little skeptical that one existed). But my brother Paul is one of those perfect men so I know they are out there. Eli can fix anything that can possibly break. He buys Jesse flowers every week and takes her on romantic weekends. Eli is a man's man who knows how to treat a lady with love and respect. Eli and Jesse are good team players and are very supportive of one another. A perfect match! Nothing could make me happier as a parent than to see my daughter in a healthy relationship. It's so refreshing to see two people so much in love with each other. I always tell my daughter that Eli is a keeper.

I had a wonderful Christmas holiday with my family in Seattle and for most of the days it was sunny. Before I knew it, it was time for me to drive home. After driving 3 days back home I needed to rethink this driving to Seattle for the holiday thing that I had going on.

During the 3-day drive from Seattle to Denver the weather was cold. The next time I feel the need for a road trip to Seattle I'm going to drive when it's warm and I have about a month of vacation. Jesse and I always keep in touch when I'm on the road and Jesse wanted to make sure that I made it home safely. I had spent my last night of travel in Fruita, CO. I was only 274 miles from Boulder. I used my iPhone to keep track of how much gas I used, how much money I spent, and where I was at on the road. That morning when I finished charging my phone it seemed to be having problems. Once I got gas and tried to enter the amount of gas and cost in my phone, it died.

I wasn't happy about having a dead iPhone but at least I was in Colorado. I hoped Jesse didn't get too worried about not being able to reach me on my phone. Six hours in the car was a short day for me but I was ready to be home. After I unloaded my car I called my daughter. Jesse had wondered why she couldn't reach me on my iPhone. She had expected me to call back when I took a break. Jesse was happy I was home and glad that my phone hadn't died at the beginning of my trip.

It was New Year's Eve day and I had just enough time to get to the Apple store before it closed. I rushed over to Flatirons Mall and the Apple tech personnel were unable to revive my iPhone. So the Apple store gave me a new iPhone. I had my iPhone only 4 months and it had already been serviced the second month I had owned it. I thought Apple technology was better than that. I began to wonder if Gil had known about my iPhone. I remembered showing my iPhone to Gil the first week I had purchased it. I'm sure he told DL I had purchased a new iPhone. I know for sure DL was able to affect me over my home phone. DL must have put a curse on my iPhone or stuck pins in a picture of an iPhone or whatever it is that witches do to mess with your life. I thought about talking to Gil about my iPhone but he was clueless when it came to DL. DL was one of his best friends. I made sure I didn't tell Gil I had to replace my iPhone. I didn't want Gil to tell DL that my iPhone died. I wouldn't let DL know of any victories over me.

Visit to the Psychic

It was the ski season of 2010 and I hadn't even pulled my skies out of my storage space to ski. It was a bad year for snow which meant plenty of man-made ice to ski on. My energy was still low and no snow gave me a good excuse not to ski. I had even called my old college roommate Linda that lived in Silverthorne and asked her if she wanted to get some spring skiing in. Linda told me not to bother. Copper Mountain was just ice; stay in Boulder and ride your bike. So I did.

One of my clients was telling me about a psychic named Linda Allen and was very impressed with her. Linda Allen is a prominent, respected physic in Denver and has written a book. Since my client just raved about Linda Allen I gave her a call to get a reading. I was curious about what she had to say about DL. What I took away from my reading with Linda made a lot of sense and provided clarity about DL. I had remarked to Linda that I usually see the darkness in people but was unable to see DL's darkness. Linda replied that DL had covered my third eye so I couldn't see DL's darkness. As far as I'm concerned DL had to be pretty powerful to cover my third eye. I still found myself longing to be friends with DL. I realized DL was still trying to compel my friendship. If DL couldn't honestly make friends with people to steal their life force, why not compel them to be your friends and then steal their life force without them knowing it? I didn't feel so stupid anymore because it took me six years to understand that DL was stealing my life force.

Knowledge is a powerful tool and I began to understand just how evil DL was and what lengths DL had gone to to steal people's life force. The daily battle drags on between us. Some days I'm DL free and other days I'm asking the higher powers every hour to cut the life force sucking cords DL uses to suck my energy. Every month I have a session with Paul and we battle DL together. I always feel my energy increase and my mind has more clarity. Paul has shared with me that black magic uses snakes to cause fear and uses spiders to cause confusion. I'm beginning to believe that DL possessed spiders to spy on me and bite me. One day I saw a black spider on the door frame. If a spider is in my apartment it's a dead spider; no questions asked. I needed to move my foot stool to stand on to reach the spider. With no intent on my part, I set the foot stool down with a loud bang. I was watching that spider and it disappeared. I just started laughing. If that spider was possessed by DL I bet it came close to having a heart attack. The rest of my day was totally DL free.

It has been two years and I'm still using the Univera products to control my over-50 womanly issues and keep my energy up. I know my vital energy percentage is on the rise and I'm enjoying living my life. I still have my bad days when I get attacked by DL. DL was a pro at inflicting great amounts of pain in my body as well as psychically getting in my head and not shutting up.

DL hooks into all my negative thoughts and makes me feel suicidal at times. I would get to the point where I was ready to do anything to stop that voice in my head. DL is good at making you think it's your voice that you're hearing, not DL's.

Weird stuff happens around the house when DL is in my head and I'm not always aware that I'm being messed with... like when my pink tourmaline necklace ended up in the wash. For some reason unknown to me I put the necklace in my pocket. I never put my necklaces in my pocket. Pink tourmaline as I wear it repairs all the holes in my aura that DL has put there. PT has a high lithium content and is calming to the wearer. When I'm calm I can shut DL out of my mind. By the time I realized where my PT necklace was, there was no necklace to save, the wire broke and all the beads went down the drain. Obviously the PT is working and DL is being blocked from putting more holes in my aura and that's why my PT necklace ended up in the wash.

Then I become frantic. I need new pink tourmaline necklaces now. I can't pick one up at Target. PT is a semi-precious stone. I had to order the beads on line and once I got the beads in the mail, then it takes me about an hour to make a new necklace. I pulled out my crystal book, *The Book of Stones* by Robert Simmons & Naisha Ahsian. I was looking up crystals in the book to see if I had any other crystals in my arsenal that would protect me from DL. My book fell open to page 401, tourmaline quartz, a crystal I had never considered for protection. When I'm struggling through my bleakest moments the higher powers always come through for me. Well, I better read what my crystal book has to say about tourmaline quartz. Tourmaline quartz: Psychic vacuum cleaner of energy field, repairs auric field, balances all chakras promoting well-being. Facilitates clear thinking. Produces a bubble of light around the body, screening out destructive energies. Ideal for psychic protection. The ability to heal rooms and environments.

I didn't have any tourmaline quartz in my arsenal but I have my sources. El Loro, a local crystal store that I have shopped at for the past 24 years on the Pearl Street Mall, might have what I need. I rushed out the front door not wanting to waste any time hoping to calm my frantic self. El Loro is my favorite crystal shop in Boulder and I spend money every time I walk through door. I asked the shop keeper if she had any tourmaline quartz jewelry. She showed me a case with only two TQ pendants. I bought the bigger of the two pendants. The shop keeper suggested I look at the tumbled TQ. As I dug through the tumbled stones of TQ my frantic self turned to a euphoric demeanor. The TQ tumbled stones were only $1-$2 a piece. I bought TQ tumbled stones for my Rolfing table, car and enough to place all over my house.

I returned home and found a silver chain for my tourmaline quartz pendant. It took me a few hours of wearing my new TQ pendant to notice that I wasn't hearing DL's voice in my head. Not really a voice but just annoying static noises. Seven years of annoying static gone from my head. It felt so good to hear the sound of silence in my head. Finally a crystal shut DL up! Within a week of wearing my new crystal the silver chain broke and I almost lost my pendant. DL didn't like being shut out of my mind. All I can say is good for me, tough cookie for DL. DL was very hot for me to lose my TQ pendant. I just needed a bigger chain and I happened to have one.

DL just can't seem to leave me alone. DL can't seem to steal enough life force from me. DL is a dark hole and no amount of light will fill the emptiness until DL finds the light. DL has let ego delude her into thinking she is serving the light. Stealing clients' life force, taking their gifts, using black magic and calling on the dark energies and dark beings to do their bidding. Wrong! Let me make this quite clear, you're not serving the higher powers. DL tells clients there is no evil. That's easy for DL to say. No ethical boundaries stop DL from ruining people's lives.

DL is still trying to help me lose my new pendant and thick silver chain. The clasp broke on my thick silver chain. I went to a crystal bead and jewelry shop on Pearl Street close to 21st. I was planning to buy and replace the broken clasp. I almost lost my tourmaline quartz pendant before I noticed that the clasp was broken. The owner of the shop kindly offered to replace the clasp for me and commented about the clasp that was on my chain, saying these clasps never break. Why does that not surprise me? A clasp that shouldn't break, breaks. The TQ must be a very powerful crystal because DL is trying so hard to remove it from around my neck.

Message from DL

The next time I see Gil he has a message from DL. DL must be desperate to get inside my head and I'm absolutely sure TQ is protecting me from DL reading my thoughts. Gil begins telling me DL's sad story about how DL has been working with a healer to clear the two beings that keep me from working with DL. Sweet Gil. He told DL all about Beth, the Rolfer I trained to work on me and how good I think her work is. Gil asked me if there was any chance that I would recommend Beth to work with DL. My replay to Gil was, I would not recommend Beth to be DL's Rolfer. But in my mind I was screaming never ever would I subject any person to DL.

I know what DL is after. DL wants a Rolfer that works in the same style I do with lots of energy to suck their life force and use Beth to get hooks back into my energy field. This is the first time DL has admitted to any of the accusations that I have made. But I know what DL is not telling anyone. DL controls the beings that possess DL and the black arts and calls on all the dark energies to suck more life force from the living, causing disease, pain and the MRSA I started having trouble with in April on my face. Leave it to a vindictive person to attack a woman's face.

Gil was interested in my touch screen computer. I couldn't resist showing Gil how fun my touch screen was to use. Gil touched the screen to see how it worked and he liked the concept of a touch screen computer. I'm sure Gil wasted no time in giving DL my answer of rejection. Gil has no idea that DL is using him. He thinks DL is this sweet person that is a great healer. I knew there would be some type of retribution from DL. No matter what, if I help or fight, DL makes me suffer. I would rather fight DL and destroy all cords and connections that have been hooked to me for the last seven years. Gil is totally unaware that he is a carrier for those dark energies. I don't understand why he is unaware and feels so unaffected by the dark energies he carries. Poor Gil is so enchanted by DL's lies he can't see who DL really is. I could always feel the dark energies; it just took me years to realize where they were coming from.

The next day after Gil's visit I felt fine but my new computer stopped working. I took in my new touch screen computer that I had owned for only four months and dropped it off at Best Buy. I had typed 40 pages of the book about the exploits of DL, 15 pages of which weren't backed up. How my psychic gifts uncover the truth about her. Best Buy was unable to recover any data from my computer. Both the mother board and the hard drive were fried. Best Buy had to send my Touch Screen back to the HP factory to have it rebuilt. I never buy warranties but my little voice was saying you need to buy a warranty for this computer. DL fried my computer but the warranty replaced it. I have the light on my side. Now I print every page after I write it. You never know when some witch might fry your computer. My rebuilt computer has its own crystals to protect it from DL and it is never on when Gil is in my office.

I shared what happened to my computer with Beth. Beth had no desire to have DL for a client and I made sure Gil or DL didn't know Beth's last name. It is hard to curse a person without knowing their full name. Beth asked me what DL's name was so she would be sure not to return any of DL's calls. Beth is an expert when it comes to computers and agreed with me that normally a computer's mother board and hard drive don't simultaneously destruct, especially when you're dealing with a new computer.

I'm wondering why I even tell Gil anything about my life these days. Perhaps I know how very angry it makes DL when I still work with Gil and won't work with DL. Even though I know I will suffer some repercussion for keeping Gil as a client and friend, I like Gil. He is just another clueless victim who has no idea who DL is. Gil made amazing homeopathic remedies and I got great results from his remedies. His $24,000 machine that he made remedies with shortly after he met DL burned up because of some strange unexplainable circumstance. He bought a new machine before he started working with me.

I'm sad to say Gil started having trouble with his new remedies machine he had purchased. Then Gil's business began to dry up and he didn't want to do the work anymore. I suspect that DL had a hand in the destruction of Gil's practice. Gil dearly loves DL and would never believe the truth about how evil this person is. I don't tell Gil because he would never believe me. It took Tim 1½ years to help me realize that DL was slowly destroying me.

The beginning of April I started having trouble with MRSA. MRSA is an antibiotic-resistant strain of staph, as if staph isn't bad enough. I'm thinking that DL is still pissed off at me for not recommending Beth to be her Rolfer. I have dealt with impetigo that I suspected its origins were from DL. DL had infected me and my chiropractor Jon with impetigo in the fall of 2007. Since Jon was helping me fight black magic from DL we both were infected with impetigo. It is not easy stuff to get rid of either. Infecting someone with a disease takes an infinite knowledge of black magic or what I like to call the dark arts. DL has no ethics and is a jealous, vindictive person who's not getting their way. My face broke out with MRSA and if that wasn't bad enough it spread to my eyes. Urgent Care is conveniently located close to my home. The doc at Urgent Care recognized that I had MRSA as soon as she saw my face. The doc gave me a prescription for two types of antibiotics and antibiotic drops for my eyes.

I had told Gil that I was planning a weekend trip to Phoenix with my daughter Jesse and her boyfriend Eli. I should know by now that when Gil comes in for a Rolfing session I need to zip it about my personal life. Gil is a stay at home dad that likes to stay in touch with the housewife network, and DL is his friend and confidant. So what I tell Gil, DL soon knows. Every time I find a crystal that protects me or destroys DL's ability to steal my vital energy DL uses another tactic. All I'm trying to do is protect myself and keep DL from killing me. Well, if DL thinks I'm going to let her destroy me, DL picked the wrong person to mess with.

The strong antibiotics that I had to take for the MRSA made me so sick I couldn't get out of bed. I got on line and checked out the side effects of the antibiotics I was taking and found I was suffering from the side effects. I cut the dose in half and then I was able to get out of bed with moderate pain. I lost 5 pounds in the week I took the antibiotics because I couldn't eat.

The MRSA cleared up on my face and body. But my eyes weren't clearing up. I had a plane ticket for Phoenix and I had to call and put my ticket on hold. I couldn't go to Phoenix until my eyes improved. Urgent Care couldn't help me but my client Deanne, a pediatrician, knew of a good optometrist. Early the next morning I called the optometrist. The optometrist had a 9 am cancellation. The receptionist told me that if I could make it to the office in 15 minutes I could have the appointment. I made it to the office in 5 minutes. The higher powers were in the game against DL. They helped me get that eye appointment. The optometrist prescribed new, just on the market, strong antibiotic eye drops. By the next day my eyes were better. Trip to Phoenix was on. The only down side was I would be driving to Phoenix, not flying. I couldn't wear any makeup because of the MRSA. Maybe it was a good thing I was driving so no one would see me in my car. At least I wouldn't have to worry about trying to look good. I have eye lashes but you can't see them without mascara. My eyes look naked because my lashes are so blonde.

Drive to Phoenix

I had two days to drive to Phoenix before Jesse and Eli would arrive from Seattle for the weekend. I always wanted to drive to Phoenix. The sun was shining but I was getting such bad gas mileage from the 60 mile per hour head winds I drove my Matrix into. Instead of 30 miles to the gallon I was getting 25. I was looking on the bright side though… I was heading for Arizona, making my way toward warm weather. As soon as I was 100 miles from Boulder I felt relief and began to feel more energy. I've always been a positive person but DL took a toll on the level of joy in my life. I was out of range of the witch's psychic energy vacuum. Great! I get to use my energy for my life instead of some witch using my energy. What a concept, I get to use my own energy!

The drive was beautiful through New Mexico. But I would never recommend spending the night in Gallup, NM. I woke to cold weather, scraped 4 inches of snow off my car and paid way too much for the dump I stayed in. Friday I drove most of the day and was elated that the high winds had ended. By mid afternoon I drove into the east side of Phoenix armed with my Garmin GPS. I found the Sheraton and scored such a great deal on room rates for the three of us for the weekend.

The Sheraton was perfect for the restful weekend I needed. All I wanted to do was lounge at the edge of the pool, soak up the sun and swim in the inviting water of the beautiful pool. I had a few hours to kill before I picked up Jesse & Eli at the airport. Everything I could want was within walking distance of the Sheraton. I could even walk to my favorite restaurant Chipotle. I finished up my early dinner and took my Matrix to the car wash. My room was beautiful, with a great view of the pool, comfy beds and I was more than ready for a hot shower.

It was late by the time I picked up Jesse and Eli at the airport but I was so happy to be with my family. Eli and Jesse were impressed with the room I had scored at the Sheraton. Eli was an architect that designed Marriott hotels so I could trust his insight concerning the value of our room. Jesse and Eli were ready for dinner and a night dip at the pool. It had been a long day for me with almost no sleep on the lumpy bed the night before. I wished Jesse and Eli a good evening and was asleep on my comfy bed instantly.

Eli got up early on Saturday morning to go fishing with his friend that lived in Phoenix. Jesse and I had the whole day to ourselves. We walked over to Mimi's for breakfast. The day was warm and sunny and I was wearing one of my summer dresses and a pair of sandals. I love Phoenix in the winter. After breakfast we walked over to the Metrocenter Mall to do a little shopping. We didn't spend much time at the Mall because our next stop would be pool side. I was dreaming of soaking up the sun. Oh wait, I'm taking antibiotics, I can't sun bathe and risk a rash all over my body. I sat under the shade umbrella with a cover up on my legs. But I was pool side and could feel the warmth of the sun through my cover up and could pretend to be sun bathing. I wouldn't give up swimming to stay out of the sun. Technically, I was under the water, not in the sun. It felt so refreshing to swim. The water felt very clean and soothing to my skin. I don't smell any chlorine so this must be a salt water pool. After swimming in a salt water pool I could never go back to a chlorinated pool. The salt water helped cleared up the rest of the MRSA on my face. I'm sure that being out of range of the witch helped my face look better too.

Eli met us at the pool after his fishing trip and took a dip in the pool with Jesse and me. Eli tasted the water and said yes, this is a salt water pool. We all agreed that salt water pools were way superior compared to chlorinated pools. What could be better than sun, blue sky, the smell of Hawaiian Tropic and swimming in a salt water pool? Well not better, but to top off the day, a tasty Mexican dinner with margaritas on the rocks with salt, within walking distance. No one had to be the designated driver, so bring on the margaritas!

Sunday our plan was to live by the pool. After breakfast Jesse and I found a Whole Foods store with my handy GPS. We bought turkey wraps and beer so we wouldn't have to leave pool side. The three of us spent another full day in the Sheraton's paradisiacal setting. I'm allergic to chlorine but the hot tub at the Sheraton was also salt water and I enjoyed every minute warming my bones before returning to Colorado. Of our group I was the only fully white person left after our weekend in the sun. Jesse and Eli had a good sun burn going by the time they were packing to leave for Seattle. Three more months of rain in Seattle before summer, Jesse and Eli were working on their sun deficit. That evening I took the kids to the airport. I was sad to see our weekend come to its end but what a great weekend we had.

Part Three — Fighting the Dark Side

I spent one last night at the Sheraton after dropping Jesse and Eli at the airport. I didn't have as much fun in paradise without my family but I wanted to leave early in the morning to start my drive back to Boulder. If it weren't for DL, I would be flying back, not driving back.

I made sure to spend the night in an uptown hotel in Albuquerque and drove past Gallup. On the drive back I stopped in the old town of Santa Fe. Santa Fe was celebrating its 400th birthday. I was unaware that Santa Fe was one of the oldest cities in America. I found a beautiful felt magenta cowgirl hat with a matching bead band. I could have this lovely cowgirl hat for only $400. It would be awhile before I saved that much money or won the lottery. I had to pass on the hat for the day. I did find a great French restaurant in Santa Fe and could afford the best egg and spinach quiche ever.

My drive back was sunny and pleasant with no head winds. I like getting 30 mpg; I only used 3 tanks of gas on the way home. What I find interesting is when I drive back to Boulder I never feel my energy drop off. But when I leave Boulder and get 100 miles away I feel my energy increase dramatically. What is it that DL does? Is it like a drop of water? One drop of water isn't much but if you have enough drops of water you can fill up a bath tub. Does DL just take one drop of energy at a time and after a long period of time takes a whole bath tub full of my energy? It's always a relief to shut off a drippy faucet. Perhaps it's more of a relief to stop losing energy all at once. It could be when I return to the witch's energy vacuum zone I don't notice a small loss of energy at first.

Energy Vampires

Boulder has a metaphysical book store downstairs on the corner of Broadway and Pearl, the only place in town to buy black candles. Black candles are good for sending evil back to dark arts practitioners. On this particular warm May day I wasn't looking for black candles; already tried that tactic with DL. I was looking for a book about energy vampires that my tarot card reader recommended I buy. I didn't find the book that Richard recommended. But I did find a book called *Psychic Vampires*, by Joe H. Slate, Ph. D. As my guiding forces would have it the article Tim had shared with me about psychic vampires was by the same author.

Pictures taken of auras during Joe Slate's research show what a healthy aura looks like and what an aura looks like after a psychic vampire attack. Puncturing occurs in the aura and tentacles from the psychic vampire absorb energy from its victim and can happen from a considerable distance. Once a hole has been made in the aura the victim's energy is drained quickly and the host becomes exhausted. Aggressive vampire attacks can cause tears to the aura.

These types of attacks are deliberately designed to inflict damage. Victims of vampire attacks feel a piercing pain at the damaged area to the aura. This discomfort can last for several days. Common side effects of a vampire attack are low energy and fatigue, a feeling that something is wrong, anxiety and a feeling of helplessness. The aura takes on a greenish gray overlay. Dealing with continuous vampire attacks can cause serious structural damage to the aura and may require a very long recovery period.

It has been almost a year since I started working with Paul Miller. We have been locked in a battle of transforming the dark energies, using love and light from the higher powers to keep DL from stealing more of my life force. Paul's work has kept DL at bay and slowly my health is being restored. I'm getting healthier, having more energy, perceiving more clarity in my thought process. I'm beginning to understand why I was feeling so much pain in my body. DL was puncturing holes in my aura and draining my energy. I could actually feel pain every time damage was caused to my aura and energy was drained from my body. Another piece of the puzzle comes into view because of Joe Slate's book about psychic vampires. The pieces fit. DL is a ravenous parasitic predator who has mastered the art form of psychic vampirism.

By the end of May I was still having issues with MRSA. I'd finished my second round of antibiotics and the MRSA on my face is still not going away. All the side effects from the antibiotics are causing me to feel worse than the MRSA itself. I'm starting to lose faith that antibiotics are the answer I'm looking for. One of my clients, Carolyn, who happens to also be my good friend, came in for a Rolfing session on the same day I'm wonder how in the world I'm going to get rid of this MRSA. Carolyn starts telling me about the Vibe machine in Cheyenne she's been using to help the inflammation in her spine. The conversation I'm having with Carolyn peaked my interest. I asked Carolyn for the number of the Vibe center in Cheyenne. I gave the center a call and asked if the Vibe can affect MRSA. I'm told that yes, MRSA can be cleared up in 3 hours.

My first day off after I talked to Carolyn I drove to Cheyenne to give the Vibe a try. After three hours of sitting by the Vibe the MRSA cleared up on my face and I noticed I had more energy. The Vibe machine is another avenue to raise my energy level so DL can't turn me into an invalid. After about a month using the Vibe my health and energy level keeps improving. During my healing session with Paul Miller I'm noticing more shifts in my energy field. Because I have more energy to work with it's harder for DL to punch holes in my aura.

I can always tell when Paul and I are making progress in our sessions against DL. Usually a member of our family will become ill with no apparent cause that can be found for the illness. Either Paul or I will become ill or a strange injury will occur to one of us. What happened on Memorial Day took us both by surprise. Paul Miller was on vacation with his family. Paul's employees were working over the Memorial Day weekend. Paul has a Christian employee, Tom, who is always teasing him about being a metaphysical teacher and healer.

Tom was watching one of his coworkers climbing up a ladder that had been used all day long at the job site. Tom watched in astonishment as he saw the end of the ladder being pulled out from under his coworker. There were no skid marks from the bottom of the ladder on the concrete floor; not even the dust was disturbed. At the next session with Paul he began telling me the story of what happened to one of his employees. The fall caused a broken facial bone and a broken arm to Paul's employee. Paul asked me if I thought DL was responsible for the injury to his employee. I pulled out my pendulum and asked the higher powers if DL was responsible for the ladder accident. Sure enough, the higher powers gave me a big yes. Paul was mad. He didn't appreciate DL attacking his employee and said if he had been on the job the accident would have never happened. Paul is a powerful healer. It's hard to believe DL went after one of his employees.

I felt really bad for Paul's injured employee and apologized saying if you weren't helping me DL wouldn't be attacking you. He assured me that she wouldn't be going after his workers anymore and no matter what happened he wouldn't back down from DL's threats. I was very grateful Paul was not intimidated by DL. Paul had been the only healer, spiritual warrior that I had worked with who was powerful enough to stop DL from destroying my health and sanity. Definitely Paul destroyed the dark energies DL filled my body with. I'm sure DL is noticing the loss of power over me and the dark energies sent to battle Paul and me. Paul has totally interfered with DL's ability to steal my life force energy. Also DL is losing the ability to affect Paul and me with dark energies. So DL goes after people in our lives that can't defend themselves from the evil. We're starting to see DL's underhanded desperation; DL is trying to intimidate us into giving up the fight. I am confident the acts of desperation against us confirm the devastating toll our interventions have caused DL's evil years of unchecked tyrannical behavior.

Isaac's Gift

The end of June my son Isaac flew down for a week visit to escape the Alaska rainy summer weather. Isaac and I had two days to ourselves. For the rest of Isaac's visit I would have to share him with his girlfriend of one year. I'm used to sharing my daughter with Eli but I've never had to share my son before. I like having my son's full attention when we are visiting. Dacia is a lovely woman and I can see she adores my son. They are a good match and are very supportive of one another. I like Dacia and feel my son is lucky to have such a sweet person in his life.

My son has the gift of seeing spirits whereas I can only feel their presence. Not that Isaac is very happy about having this gift. But he is learning to deal with it. I was telling Isaac that entities love to live in our intestines and live off the energy there. Isaac was saying OK mom. The next morning when Isaac got up he said he saw a dark energy being and it went right for his intestines, that it doesn't feel good and would you please clear me. So I took out my pendulum and cleared the dark being out of Isaac's 3rd chakra. I call the 3rd chakra the power chakra. Entities also feed off the energy from your chakras. I'm sure the dark energy or being that Isaac saw was from DL. DL likes to use dark beings to steal life force from its host. Then uses the host to steal energy from any person they come in contact with.

I was not happy at all that DL was going after my son the first night of his visit. But once I cleared DL's dark energy from Isaac's intestines he felt much better. Isaac is blessed with huge amounts of energy. Without DL's interference our combined energies were enough to protect us from her energy stealing ways for the rest of my son's visit.

Dacia arrived and joined Isaac on his vacation. Dacia and Isaac started calling my home the spa. Every morning they would sunbathe by the pool soaking up as much sun as possible. They were pretty sun starved from the rainy summer Anchorage was having. The fact that the days were hot enough to swim in the pool made lying by the pool even more inviting in the morning. The morning swim was usually followed by breakfast at Foolish Craig's Café on Pearl Street. The breakfast at Foolish Craig's was a big hit for Dacia and Isaac because they savor good food. One afternoon we took a hike from Chautauqua Park to NCAR where we had lunch that my son made. It turned out to be a 4 mile hike in the heat of the afternoon. I was teasing the kids if the heat was too much for them we could take a taxi back to Chautauqua. On our third day out we road bikes to Chipotle for dinner. I wanted to make sure I burned enough calories before eating dinner so I suggested riding the bike instead of driving to dinner. My son's visit wouldn't be complete without a Rolfing session. I didn't want Dacia to feel left out so she enjoyed having a Rolfing session also. Sunburned and well feed Isaac and Dacia were reluctant to leave the sunny days in Colorado to return back to the rain in Anchorage. They assured me they would be back.

I spent the month of July driving to Wyoming to get my energy fix from the Vibe machine. The weekly visits to the Vibe machine were great for raising my energy level and improving my health. I noticed half way to Wyoming I could feel a weight lifting off me. I felt more energy and a lot happier. I was driving out of range from DL's psychic vampire abilities. Would it be possible for DL to be stealing life force from people in a 50 mile radius? That wouldn't be a good thing. But driving 200 miles round trip once a week to Wyoming was getting old even if it did get me out of range from the psychic vampire. I ended up finding a Vibe machine in North Boulder and as long as I was sitting by the Vibe machine DL couldn't drain my energy. I was still getting my energy fix, saving the environment and spending less money on gas. A win/win situation for me.

Gil tells me during his next Rolfing session that DL has Parkinson's disease. I know that DL is one of Gil's best friends. The nicest thing I could think of to say was that's too bad and sorry to hear DL is ill. All I can think about is when Paul teases me and tells me if DL were to cross over she would be a lot easier to deal with. I absolutely couldn't muster up any compassion for that person. DL loves it when people feel sorry for her because that's the best time to ask people for their energy for healing. No one can heal a black hole whose ego has deluded them so badly that they've lost their connection to the higher powers. I'm sure DL is looking for some kind of response from me. My plan is to never have anything to do with that person the rest of my life. I will be experiencing ripples of revenge for not feeling any compassion for DL or someone I know will. Or my face is going to break out more than it's already done. Before I met DL my face never broke out. Witch, can you just leave the face alone?

The next thing you know I find out my daughter is on antidepressants. Jesse tells me that her job is so stressful she is starting to have anxiety attacks driving to work. The anxiety is so bad she can't get her work done. It's bad enough that my daughter is taking anxiety medicine but now her face is breaking out also. For the moment all I could think to do was keep clearing and send her a necklace of black jade to protect her from energy vampires.

The Proposal

In September Jesse told me of Eli's plans for a romantic weekend of wine tasting and a walk about the vineyards in Wenatchee. I'm sure the weekend will help both Jesse and Eli's stress levels. Eli and Jesse were exploring the vineyards eating grapes off the vine and tasting wine. Eli determined he needed to pop the question before Jesse had tasted too much wine. Eli kneeled in the miles of scenic rows of ripe grapes and asked Jesse for her hand in marriage. Jesse was so taken aback by Eli's proposal that she grabbed the ring, slid it on her finger and became mesmerized by the sight of the ring on her finger. Eli asked is that a Yes? Yes, replied Jesse. She threw her arms around Eli and began to cry. Jesse my wonderful daughter called me first.

I called my son Isaac and told him of the good news. According to Isaac I wasn't the first person to know about Jesse's proposal. Isaac and his girlfriend Dacia were up at the grandparents' house for dinner the night Eli called and asked George's permission to marry his granddaughter. George was excited about Jesse getting married and was about to give her a call and express his congratulations. Isaac caught George before he could give Jesse a call. "George, don't call Jesse; she doesn't know Eli is going to propose. You will ruin the surprise for her." My amazing son saves the day for his sister.

I was so happy for my daughter I began to cry. My daughter

was marrying her match. Everyone could see how much in love they were. All my relatives feel certain their love will last. As a parent I want to see both my children happily married. One down; one to go. I love Eli; he will be the best son-in-law ever. Eli and Jesse are very supportive and caring of one another. Eli & Jesse will take care of each other and have an amazing life together.

My plan was to visit Jesse on my birthday and go out with the family to my favorite restaurant, Bahama Breeze. Jesse asked me, "I know it's your birthday but would you mind looking at wedding dresses that weekend?" I said I would love to shop for wedding dresses while I'm in Seattle. Then my brother asked if I would Rolf a few of his friends while I was down for my birthday and I said, "Why not?" It would give me extra spending money while I was in Seattle. A little extra for Jesse and me because we love shopping together in Seattle. I'm so excited about Jesse's engagement and to see her ring. But I worried about the anxiety she was having. This is not normal for my daughter to have anxiety; I'm very perplexed by this turn of events. What am I missing here? I cleared my son, daughter and family every day. The next session I have with Paul I'll ask him to see what could be affecting my daughter in this bizarre manner.

Visit to Mesa Verde

This year of 2010 on my birthday I turn 55 years old. That makes this birthday special for me and I want to make a week long celebration of my birthday this year. The weekend before I head off to Seattle my plan is to stay with an old friend in Durango and visit Mesa Verde. PJ, my dear friend of 26 years that I skied with in Alaska, offered to be my tour guide in Mesa Verde. Ever since I moved to Boulder I've wanted to visit Mesa Verde. Another thing I can cross off my list before I die. I love it when a plan comes together. I spent Saturday driving 6 hours to meet Paul at Pagosa Springs, another place I had on my list to visit in Colorado. I love Mexican food and right across the river from the hot springs was Tequilas. I was starving so PJ and I had yummy Mexican food and margaritas. What a great way to start my birthday week. The Pagosa Hot Springs are beautiful and nothing feels better than a hot soak after sitting 6 hours in the car. After catching up on years gone by and a two hour soak testing the water in as many pools that had the right temperature we still had an hour drive to Durango.

I was a happy camper to finally arrive at PJ's home and more than ready to be out of my car. Upon entering PJ's home I noticed a massage table set up in his living room. I asked PJ if that was some kind of a hint. PJ said he had the table set up for his daughter. Since PJ was providing me with weekend accommodations it was the least I could do so I gifted PJ with some Rolfing. While I was Rolfing and we were talking I plugged my iPhone into his stereo so we could listen to the new John Mayer and Dave Matthews albums. I shared with PJ how my life was affected by DL and that Paul Miller, my healer, was helping me clear the dark energy out of my body from DL. PJ asked what I did with spirits or beings when I felt them. Last year I had given PJ a quartz crystal on a chain that he could wear but also use as a pendulum. That evening I taught PJ how to clear spirits and change energy with his pendulum.

Sunday we had a short road trip to Mesa Verde, only about an hour drive. We stopped at the local coffee shop to buy turkey sandwiches for our lunch at Mesa Verde. Our first stop at Mesa Verde was Chapin Mesa Museum where we bought tickets for the Cliff Palace tour. Tourists are only allowed in Cliff Palace with a park ranger guide. We had a few hours before the guided tour of Cliff Palace started. We had plenty of time to visit Spruce Tree House on our own self-guided walking tour. It's an easy hike down to visit Spruce House and probably one of the most accessible ruins to walk to.

As we began exploring the ruins we both could feel the energetic presence of spirits all around us. Then we climbed down a ladder into a kava. PJ felt a heavy weight on his body and his knees almost gave way. I also felt the extra weight of all the spirits surrounding us in the underground kava. I left the kava almost as soon as I arrived at the bottom of the ladder. Not really interested in taking any pictures as I hurried back up the ladder to escape the overwhelming spirit energies. I was excited that PJ could feel the same spirits I could feel.

Not many people I know can share that experience with me. Even though I have been dealing with this phenomenon for many years it's always nice to get some validation from another person. I don't tell many people of my ability to feel and talk with spirits. I don't feel comfortable when people view me as a nut case. We didn't share our discoveries with the park ranger; we just kept the information to ourselves. Once we got far enough away from Spruce Tree House and weren't being overwhelmed by spirits, I began helping the spirits that came with us to cross over into the light so we could hold on to our life force energy. The spirits we encountered at the Spruce House were all pretty nice spirits and just wanted help to cross over into the light. Somehow spirits know I can help them and they stay with me until I help them cross over.

Next stop, Cliff Palace. We showed up early to have lunch and fill our Camelbacks with water for the tour. We are both such good prepared campers. PJ and I talked about how spirit guides can give you answers while using a pendulum. PJ wanted to ask his spirit guides some questions using his pendulum about the Ancestral Puebloans while we were at the ruins of the Cliff Palace. The tour began with a view from above the Cliff Palace. We can see the people in Cliff Palace taking the tour before us. When the tour finished below us, it was our turn to descend down the steep cliff side on narrow steps carved out of the sandstone.

Before we could enter the Cliff Palace the ranger gave a short lecture and offered a question and answer period. PJ was trying his hand at using his pendulum. "Gwin, my pendulum is not working." I replied, "Choose your questions wisely. Don't anger your spirit guides. Apologize to your spirit guides." PJ took my advice to heart and his spirit guides allowed the pendulum to answer his questions. Question and answer period over, we began the tour of the Cliff Palace. I kept trying to visualize what Cliff Palace would have looked like at its peak of existence. No luck. I couldn't see a thing. But it did seem like we were dealing with more spirit energies than we had perceived at Spruce House. The building skills of the Ancestral Puebloans were amazing. Wow, this construction reminds me of condos. These Indians built the first condo complexes. Leaving the Cliff Palace I found to be more challenging than descending the steep steps. The group had to climb through a tall crevice in the sandstone and climb up a tall ladder to reach the rim of the canyon. Since I have a fear of heights the climb up the ladder was the exciting high point of the tour for me.

I for one couldn't wait to get away from the crowd. News must travel fast from one dwelling to the next in the spirit world. I must have had more than 100 spirits around me waiting to cross over. I wasted no time in crossing over the spirits surrounding PJ and me. There is always a spirit who is not ready to cross over but wants to experience life through your body. PJ and I had just had lunch before the tour yet I was ravenously hungry. That's a dead giveaway that you have just been possessed by a spirit who wants to experience human feeling again. I remember the first time I ate a jar of green olives before I realized that it wasn't me who wanted to eat a jar of green olives. While I wasn't feeling so well I had my spirit guides help me cross over this green olive eating spirit before I could buy another jar of green olives. While the spirit possessed me, the green olives tasted so good. I always travel with 7 stones of tourmaline quartz in a small crystal bag. When the occasion arises and I have a stubborn spirit who wants to set up house in my body, I rub the bag of TQ in a circle on the palm of my hand that pulls the spirit out of my body and I have my spirit guides return the spirit back to where it came from or help the spirit cross over. No surprise to me, after I evicted my spirit guest I was no longer hungry.

PJ asked if I wanted to see any more sights while we were at Mesa Verde. No, I think I'm done. I'm ready for a bike ride before dinner. I would like to burn off some calories and recharge my battery. I've visited with more than enough spirits for today. On the drive back I experience bliss. What I mean when I say bliss is when I become connected to the higher powers so completely it becomes blissful. I find myself in a total state of happy contentment, making it hard to carry on a coherent conversation with PJ. Before PJ thinks I'm a total idiot I better explain what I'm experiencing. PJ, you know all the spirits I helped cross over today. They are expressing their gratitude because I asked my spirit guides to help them cross over. The gift from the spirits to me is a direct connection to the love and light. I didn't even have to meditate for years or meditate at all to experience enlightenment. That's what I call the Bliss; total hook up with the love and light from the source. PJ drove back to Durango and what a blissful drive it was for me. By the time we pulled into the driveway my battery was charged and I was ready for that scenic bike ride along the river bike trail through Durango.

PJ and I changed into biking apparel and made sure the mountain bike tires had enough air. We biked from Paul's house to the bike trail along the river. What a beautiful fall evening with trees colored in reds and yellows. The rivers in Colorado have always invited me to take off my shoes and dangle my feet in the clear water that allow you to see the river bed of rocks. But on a fall October evening I would be content with the magical energy I could feel from the water riding my bike along its banks. I swear we biked 20 miles that evening but PJ said it was only 15. It felt like 20 miles to me trying to keep up with PJ. I enjoyed a lovely sunset while riding back as temperatures began to fall. We managed to pull our bikes into the drive before the light of the day was totally gone.

After burning off about 800 calories I was ready for dinner and another birthday toast. Happy Birthday to me! I hadn't made any plans for dinner, so PJ and I walked along old Main Street of Durango seeing what moved me for dinner. I caught sight of the Strater Hotel and fell in love with the Victorian style hotel. They say the hotel is haunted. Oh great! The dining area looked charmingly beautiful and the food should be fabulous. I usually pick a restaurant by how good the energy feels when I enter the room. Most of the time I can tell by the energy in the room if the service will be good, if the food will be good and if I will have a pleasant dining experience.

My pick was the Strater Hotel for dinner. I would take my chances with any spirits I encountered at dinner. PJ agreed the food was probably the best in town. The atmosphere, food, company and service exceeded my expectations. I toasted my 55th birthday with champagne. What I didn't expect was the vision of all the happy spirits dining with us. The room was full of happy couples in Victorian dress dining with the present day patrons.

I remarked to PJ that I had never been in a room with so many happy spirits in my life. The spirits liked our energy and were trying their hand at match making. I was relieved that I was the only one who could hear what the spirits were saying. PJ and I had been friends for years. I didn't want to destroy our friendship by trying to turn our friendship into a relationship. PJ was still recovering from being dumped by the love of his life. I survived dinner without being possessed and had the most romantic birthday dinner with the blessings of the spirits.

PJ wanted to go upstairs and see what spirits we could feel. I was thinking why temp fate? I just had a lovely dinner. I reluctantly agreed and we climbed the staircase to the second floor and then to the third floor. There was no way I could climb another flight of stairs; I was frozen not wanting to go any farther. I could feel all the spirits leaning over the railing of the staircase all the way to the top floor watching us. PJ and I were overwhelmed with spirits. I started freezing, a sure sign the spirits were pulling energy away from us. All the hairs on the back of PJ's neck were standing on end. We managed to find the spirits that weren't so happy being stuck on the earthly plan. I told PJ I needed to leave now. PJ replied, "I think I have felt enough spirit energy for the evening." PJ and I left through the bar and the level overlooking the bar was full of celebrating spirits. Haunted? That's quite the understatement. The Strater Hotel is a spirit resort! Once we were on Main Street out of view of other guests I began helping spirits cross over so I could warm up. As I looked back at the Strater Hotel I could see spirits hanging out of the windows waving us farewell. What a fun loving group of spirits.

It was comforting to be back at PJ's spirit free home. PJ had a friend come over to his house and burn sage throughout his home to encourage all his spirit guests to leave. I was all for hanging out on the leather sofa and listening to music. I was ready to enjoy a restful calm evening and take a break from the long day of spirit encounters. PJ's home was very cozy and he had done a great job of remodeling the house after he bought it.

PJ started sharing with me the trouble he was having getting over his terminated relationship. I began to suspect he might be dealing with an energy vampire. These are the questions I ask when I suspect energy vampirism.

> Has your health declined during the relationship?
> Has your prosperity declined?
> Do you no longer have the energy to get things done?
> Do you still care for this person even though they used you?
> Did you offer to give this person energy?

Mr. PJ, I can feel from your aura that your heart has been broken. Judging from the huge hole behind your heart chakra I'm quite certain you're dealing with an energy vampire. My healer, Paul Miller, had repaired the holes in my aura from DL. I was willing to try my hand at aura repair. I could feel a lack of energy with my hands where the holes were located in PJ's energy field. I channeled the healing energy of the creative powers of the universe with my hands to restore the light to PJ's energy field where the hole had been. I also repaired a huge gaping hole in the front of the aura causing PJ to lose energy from his power chakra.

After I repaired the holes in PJ's aura he immediately felt his energy increase. Next on my list was to cut and destroy all energy vampire cords that were stealing life force energy from him. I asked the higher powers to cut all energy vampire cords attached to PJ from his ex. PJ felt another increase in his energy. Paul had offered to give his ex all the energy she wanted. PJ, you need to use your pendulum to break the contract you made with her. PJ used his pendulum and asked the higher powers to break the contract he had made letting a certain person use his energy. Once the contract was broken PJ felt his energy increase again.

PJ, I think you're all clear of the energy vampire. Now PJ would be able to use his own energy to help heal the damage in his body from an old injury. I would have more energy to work with to shift the imbalances in his structure so the nerves and tissue could heal. While PJ was on the massage table he began to feel the energy vampire trying to steal his energy. I instructed PJ on ways to prevent an energy vampire from stealing energy. PJ felt an energetic shift in the way he viewed the relationship he had been in. PJ replied, "I'm starting not to care for that person." Energy vampires are talented when it comes to compelling people to like them so they can continue to steal their life force. PJ couldn't put his finger on what was wrong but now he knows he was a victim of an energy vampire.

PJ wanted to work on creating more prosperity in his life using the pendulum. So we worked on shifting the energy in his life and clearing any blockage that kept PJ from being prosperous. Time for me to hit the hay. Monday morning we had breakfast on Main Street in Durango. I had only one encounter that morning with a spirit while trying to leave the diner. The spirit caught my coat on a hook on my way through the door. The spirit was just having some fun with me. But I'm sure PJ thought I was a klutz. I thanked Paul for celebrating my birthday with me. I let PJ know that he had made my 55th birthday special and I had a great time in Durango.

I spent three days with PJ and helped him deal with an energy vampire. My healer, Paul Miller, told me during one of my first sessions the reason I was dealing with so much evil was to teach me how to use my gifts. I could see clearly what PJ was trying to tell me. I was able to help my dear friend gain liberation from a destructive energy vampire. My healer said I had to write my book to free myself from the destructive energies of DL. I could also see that my book would help others to gain their life back from energy vampires. That's when I (not having any skills as a writer) got serious about getting this book written.

55th Birthday in Seattle

I drove the long 7-hour trek back to Boulder and was home 2 days before I caught a plane for Seattle. I flew in Thursday night and Jesse and Eli picked me up at the airport. Friday morning I was up at 6 am. Jesse dropped me off at the Fauntory Ferry, which works out great for me because I don't need a car to get to my brother's house and I never have to wait in line with my car to get on the ferry. I love riding the ferry over to my brother's. The waters are calming and energizing at the same time. Paul picked me up at Southworth and I had five of my brother's friends to Rolf before I took the 1 pm ferry back to meet Jesse and shop for her wedding dress.

My brother and I have always been super close and have the same convictions about alternative health choices. His friends weren't having any luck getting rid of their SI and back pain. Paul asked me if I could remedy the problem. Sounds like your friends' sacrums are out of place which is causing nerve impingement. From the time I arrived I worked nonstop on one person after another. Everyone I worked on felt better after their first session. I let them know it would take more organization of the tissue before the sacrum would stay in place. Some problems only take one session to shift the tissue for a permanent change. Once the change occurs the pain is gone. Five clients done and my brother dropped me off at the ferry. I gave my brother a big hug and said I'd be back Saturday morning. Love you!

I met Jesse at the ferry pickup and we were off to look at wedding dresses. Jesse picked up Sara at her home, her best friend from 2nd grade. Jesse had a 3 pm appointment to try on wedding dresses in downtown Seattle. I've heard said that it's the clothing that makes the person. But in Jesse's case any dress she tried on looked like a million bucks. We started at the most expensive bridal shop in Seattle. The dresses were all exquisite and Jesse fell in love with a dress that made her feel beautiful. The dress was only $5,000. But Jesse knew the type of dress she was looking for now. We started

Part Three   **Fighting the Dark Side**

with the pricey dresses and it was time to work our way down to the more affordable dresses. We visited three more affordable dress shops that day but no dresses gave Jesse the beautiful vibes. So Jesse had appointments to look at dresses on Saturday.

Saturday was another early morning trip on the ferry to Port Orchard. I Rolfed three clients and visited with my dad and brother. Then we caught the ferry back to Fauntory to meet Jesse and watch her try on more wedding dresses. Our next destination was dress shops located in the South Center area. At the affordable dress shops I could take pictures of all the dresses that Jesse tried on and see how they looked in the photo. We both wanted a dress that would look good and be slimming in the wedding photos. A few of the dresses I thought looked great but after viewing the photo of the dress, it was the opposite of slimming. I should bring a camera along when I'm trying on clothing. It would save me the time of returning items that didn't accentuate my figure. Taking pictures of the dresses saves time and trying to remember what each dress looked like. No dresses made the cut on Saturday.

Saturday night my family celebrated my 55th birthday with me at the Bahama Breeze. My brother, his wife, Jesse & Eli are always fun to party with. The food is amazing and the mashed yams with cinnamon are one of my favorite side dishes. We were seated in the atrium with live Caribbean music. The restaurant reminds me of my Caribbean trip to Belize. They served juicy tropical drinks with rum that didn't taste like they had alcohol in them. It was a great evening and I didn't have to drive home. It was the first time I spent a week celebrating my birthday. It was a great way to celebrate life with friends and family.

Sunday I enjoyed sleeping in late and going out for coffee with Jesse. We did make one more stop to look at dresses but nothing caught Jesse's interest. I feel very blessed to have a loving family that loves me. I'm wealthy beyond measure because of the close relationships I share with my family. I always tell my children they are my treasure in this life. I had plenty of energy to enjoy my family because I was far away from DL and being with my family is always energizing.

The Wedding Dress

The next day I was back home in Boulder and that Monday afternoon I had an appointment with Paul Miller. I asked Paul if there was any way he could help my daughter. Paul answered, "Let me take a look and see what I can do for Jesse." Paul took a psychic look at what was going on in Jesse's life. Paul could see that a huge amount of energy was being drained from Jesse at her office. Paul psychically began laying down an energy protective grid in Jesse's office to protect her from life force drainage that had been causing her so much stress and anxiety. I thanked Paul and didn't give another thought to the session after I left.

John, one of my brother's friends that I had worked on, wanted to fly out to Boulder and try some more Rolfing. After one Rolfing session John felt the first pain relief he had in many months. We began discussing the cost of John flying to Boulder and paying for a hotel. My suggestion was why don't you pay my way to Seattle because I have a place to stay and don't need to rent a car. I can work on you at my brother's house and you will save lots of money and a big bonus, you don't have to deal with the new airport scanners. My brother is great at finding deals on airline tickets. So Paul set up my flight for November 13th. I hadn't planned to be back in Seattle in less than 4 weeks. I hoped my daughter didn't mind putting me up for a couple of nights and picking me up at the airport. I was relieved to hear that Jesse was excited that I was coming out to visit her so soon. Jesse said she would set up some more appointments to try on wedding dresses.

The day I called Jesse to let her know I would be seeing her in November, Jesse said she had set up an appointment to try on dresses that day in a shop located close to Green Lake. Gwen, a friend of Jesse's that she worked with, was planning to go with her. However, the day of her appointment she was so stressed out that all she wanted to do was go home and sleep. Jesse let Gwen know that she needed to reschedule her appointment. Jesse was in no mood to try on wedding dresses. That is unusual for Jesse who

Part Three   **Fighting the Dark Side**

never turns down an opportunity to go clothes shopping. Jesse shared with me that it worked out for the best that she didn't go shopping with Gwen. "I'm glad you're flying back out to Seattle. I would much rather go shopping for wedding dresses with you, Mom." I was delighted that my daughter had no problem with me being back in Seattle so soon. I would never want to be an imposition for my daughter.

I arrived back in Seattle Friday night; Jesse and Eli picked me up at the airport. I can always tell when my daughter has been crying; her eyes get puffy. Jesse, have you been crying? Not only had Jesse been crying all day she was having an emotional melt down. Jesse told me that her friend at work had been caught committing fraud. But Gwen had made it look like Jesse committed the fraud. Wow, was all I could say. But I was thinking, shit has hit the fan at Jesse's office. Jesse was freaking out and thinking she was going to lose her job. But Jesse's boss was on her side and only time would tell how things would work out. Jesse had some wine to calm down. That evening Jesse and Eli went out with friends to have some more wine. I told Jesse might as well enjoy the weekend.

It was an early Saturday morning for me catching the ferry to Port Orchard to work. I planned three Rolfing sessions for John, one session a day to keep the pain away. John asked if I could work on his girlfriend so I squeezed her in. John's girlfriend was an easy fix, one session. The mornings I saw clients at my brother's and the afternoons I spent with my daughter.

Jesse loves Thai food. We stopped in Freemont Saturday to have lunch and enjoy some of the best Thai food that I have ever had. The Thai restaurant happens to be just down the street from a cake bakery. When Jesse lived in Queen Ann she would walk over and buy a slice of this amazing cake. Mom, you will love this cake. I had never seen pumpkin cake with cream cheese icing before. I bought a slice of pumpkin cake and Jesse picked out lemon cake with coconut icing.

Saturday afternoon we met up with Sara and drove to the dress shop in Green Lake. Jesse had found a dress online and she had printed a copy of the dress and carried it around in her purse. Jesse had called this bridal shop and they had the dress in stock that she wanted to try on. I took pictures of all the dresses she tried on that day. At the end of her appointment the mermaid wedding gown was the one she fell in love with. That must have been why she carried the picture around in her purse for days; it was her dress. Jesse looked stunning in the dress. That would be the dress Jesse would be wearing on her wedding day.

That evening Jesse and I had planned a relaxing movie night watching the large flat screen at her home. For dinner we had leftover Thai food and the most decadent cake I had ever eaten. After finding the perfect wedding dress, Jesse and I also shopped for some wine to go with our dinner celebration. A lovely colored bottle of wine caught my attention; it was a bottle of cranberry wine. The wine was made from 100% cranberries and I couldn't resist trying some. Eli was having a boys evening out but would be joining us later. Seattle has amazing restaurants with food that makes my mouth feel like it is experiencing nirvana. Not only was the leftover Thai food and cake amazing, but the cranberry wine was out of this world...the taste had such a balance of flavor and color that my taste buds fell in love. I can't remember what movie we watched but the food was unforgettable.

Sunday morning I had one more round of Rolfing sessions to go. I had an hour before I started work after getting off the ferry at Southworth so I walked the 1.4 miles to Paul's house. My day always goes better when I get some exercise. My brother would be working but I had one more session with John and I got his sacrum to shift. John was finally out of pain. I did have time to work on my dad that Sunday. My dad is always asking me to move to Seattle so I can work on him more often. Yes Dad, I would like to spend more time with my family here in the Northwest. But I love the sunshine in Colorado, and the skiing and biking that goes with the warm weather. I do enjoy the rainy weather and greenery when I visit. My face, skin and hair feel wonderfully hydrated.

After I finished working on my dad we went out to lunch. I enjoyed spending some Father/Daughter time. We went to his restaurant of choice so Dad could have some chicken fried steak. It didn't matter to me which restaurant we ate at; I had my dad all to myself for 2 hours. Dad dropped me back at my brother's house after our meal and he headed home.

I had a full day at my brother's house and my daughter would pick me up at the Fauntleroy Ferry after she got off work. Karen gave me a ride to the ferry. A blustery storm had moved in, not good weather to walk back to the ferry in. It was the first time I had ridden the ferry and seen white caps on the water. First time I felt the movement of the ferry being affected by the high winds. Walking from the ferry across the dock the wind almost blew me over. I was so happy I bought a new down coat and wore it to Seattle. Even though the wind was ferocious I was toasty warm. I was standing outside in the wind for 15 minutes while I waited for Jesse to pick me up. Jesse was worried that I would be frozen by the time she picked me up. Mom, I'm sorry I didn't get here as quickly as I thought I could after work. How are you doing? Not to worry, my sweet girl, I'm totally comfortable and toasty warm. Jesse and I had time to stop by her house, grab my luggage and rush to the airport. I gave my daughter a big hug, told her, "I love you" and rushed into the airport so I wouldn't start crying.

Lesson of the 3 Beings

It was the first week of December and my niece Nicole had been ill. She had ended up in the hospital 3 different times with her stomach hurting. After a barrage of tests including taking a look at her stomach, they were thinking she might have an ulcer. The docs did find her stomach to be oozy but didn't find an ulcer. Still not sure what was causing the problem the docs wanted to do some more tests. In the mean time I suggested Nicole take some Univera aloe for her stomach. Nicole tried the aloe and the pain went away in her stomach. My brother wasn't interested in any more tests for

Nicole and Nicole wasn't either since the aloe stopped her pain and she could keep her food down. My brother wanted to send Nicole to Denver and have me drive her to Cheyenne to try the Vibe machine.

The day before Nicole arrived, Beth was scheduled for a session and I would be working on her. Beth had started flying to Wisconsin once a month to work a week and Rolf 20 clients. Doing that many clients in a week is hard on your body. Beth would be sure to schedule an appointment with me after her week workathon so I could put her back together and relieve the pain in her body. This month Beth came in for a session after she had rolfed 23 clients in Wisconsin with a bad headache. She said it felt like her cranial bones were being pushed from the inside out. I started working on Beth and it felt like something was keeping the tissue from releasing. I retrieved my pendulum and began clearing Beth of entities and beings she had picked up from her clients in Wisconsin. After I cleared Beth she began to feel better immediately so I started working the tissue again and the tissue was softer and changed easily. Beth left and after her session I started having the same headache that she came in with. My head was so painful it felt like my cranial bones were being pushed out from the inside.

Whatever being that I had cleared from Beth was taking up residence in me. The being was stubborn and didn't want to leave or cross over. I pulled out the big gun my 4 inch crystal ball. Beings love shiny, clear, crystal balls. I laid down and had the crystal ball touch the part of my body that was in pain and waited for the being to enter the crystal ball. Once I felt the life draining energy being leave my body and enter the crystal I asked the higher powers and my arch angels to pull the being out of my crystal ball and take it over to the other side. Once the being was taken away by the higher powers my pain left with it. This being was difficult to evict from my body. It took me about an hour to clear this being even with the help of the higher powers. I'm learning that beings can cause pain in my client's body and also in my body. It's not an enjoyable lesson for me to learn.

My brother is a big believer in alternative treatments so he put his daughter on a plane to Boulder. Sunday evening I picked up Nicole at the airport. Monday morning Nicole and I drove to Wyoming to meet Gary and see what results Nicole would get with one treatment of the vibe. Nicole's stomach felt better as soon as her energy increased from the vibe machine. We were at Gary's for only an hour but Nicole stoped having pain in her stomach. We thanked Gary and Nicole slept as I drove back to Boulder that afternoon. After Nicole rested from her energizing treatment from the Vibe, that evening I rolfed her arm and neck. After I finished relieving some tightness from Nicole's arm and neck I felt extreme pain in my stomach. So I pulled out my pendulum to check if I had in fact picked up a being from Nicole that had been one of the causes of her stomach pain. Sure enough I had picked up Nicole's being. It took me about 30 minutes to clear that being from my stomach using my crystal ball and pendulum calling on all the help I could get from the higher powers asking for love and light. Finally I was cleared with welcomed help from my spirit guides. My stomach was free of pain. No wonder Nicole didn't feel well. She ended up in the hospital with huge amounts of pain. Early Tuesday morning I took Nicole back to DIA and Nicole caught her plane to Seattle. Before catching her plane Nicole told me she felt great. I'm realizing how powerful beings can be and what damage they can cause to a physical body.

That evening I had Mike for a client. He is one of my monthly clients and has been able to get off his pain meds because of the decompression properties of the Rolfing work. Mike was giving me his usual run down of his progress from his last session. Mike said he never thought she would ever get rid of my back pain. After his last session he finally noticed after a couple of weeks that he didn't have back pain any more. Today Mike just had a little sciatic pain on the right side. After Mike's rolfing session he didn't have pain on his right side at all. Mike felt so good from the session that after he got dressed and paid me, he gave me a hug of gratitude. Mike went on his merry holiday way feeling better but, my back and kidneys began to hurt. How frustrating, I must have picked up a being from Mike when he gave me a hug.

I was really having trouble shaking this being and all the time I'm in extreme pain, it makes it hard to think at all. The being didn't want to cross over and was making it difficult for me to think clearly. To clear this being, it would take more energy. I lit a candle to call the energy of love and light from the higher powers to protect me. Then I created a circle of 7 tourmaline quartz stones that represented the 7 chakras to encircle me in a circle of light and truth. Then I put my large tourmaline quartz crystal and a sphere of black tourmaline in the center of the circle with me. The black tourmaline sphere protects my energy field against beings staying attached to my aura and sucking my life force. I also used garnet in the circle to call on the creative power of the universe.

As I sat in the circle I began to feel an energy shift. I was gaining energy and the pain began to diminish. I started chanting and used my pendulum to shift the energy of the being, calling on the higher powers to fill me and my crystal circle with love and light. Then I chanted, " ill me with love and light. Turn the being to ash." The energy shifted and the being was no more. With the being destroyed my pain was gone, my energy returned, and my body temperature warmed up. Understanding crossed my mind, the higher powers were teaching me how to rid myself of dark beings. In less than a week I had experienced how dark beings cause pain and disease.

The higher powers were giving me insight into how DL used beings to do bidding. DL's use of the dark arts gave the ability to manipulate being's to do bidding. Did DL realize that sharing the body with two beings would eventual destroy health? Was DL so addicted to having power over others that DL was willing to destroy its own health for it? Gil had told me DL was suffering from Parkinson's disease and had been in pain for many years. My theory is sharing your body with beings causes energy drain and disease no matter what contract you make with them. That would explain the reason why DL is such an aggressive energy vampire. DL and the beings need energy to survive. They feel entitled and obviously have no remorse in destroying anyone's health. Perhaps the higher powers aren't so inclined to support DL's destructive dark energies anymore. Could it be that's why Paul Miller and I have been learning lessons, to hone our gifts, to battle darkness with love and light?

Where did the year go? It's already the week of Christmas 2010. I took four days off to ski and enjoy some biking. What I noticed was after 4 days off my energy was so high I felt like I was in my 30's again. I was gaining health but I still wasn't a 100 percent. I clear before I work on a client and I clear after I work on a client. DL somehow has been stealing my energy while I'm working and most likely stealing energy from my clients. Not only is DL using my energy to feed itself and the beings but can use my own energy to steal energy from others around me. Who knows how many people DL steals life force from every day?

What I'm learning is if I ask the higher powers to heal me and fill me with love and light DL can't hook into me. When I ask the higher powers to send DL love and light it blocks DL's ability to steal life force. If all of DL's victims were conscious of DL stealing their life force and in turn send DL love and light, she would never be able to steal life force again.

Since my niece's visit in December I would text her every couple of weeks to see how she was doing. I sent Nicole a text the third week in February to see how her stomach was doing. She was feeling better, hanging out with her boyfriend and watching a movie that evening at her apartment. I finished my correspondence with Nicole and my stomach started hurting. Right away I knew that the being that was causing Nicole's stomach pain was coming from her boyfriend.

I Gathered up my crystals and started clearing the stomach being from her boyfriend. Well I felt much better and I hoped Nicole felt better also. Within just a few days my brother Paul called me and told me Nicole's boyfriend broke off the relationship. Nicole was broken hearted. I felt bad for interfering and not asking permission to clear this stomach being from Nicole. I was sure the reason Nicole's boyfriend broke off the relationship was because I had threatened the being, telling the being the higher powers would destroy the being if it didn't leave Nicole alone. Another lesson learned dealing with being. You can never be sure of the outcome when you're dealing with a being that doesn't want to cross over and insists on taking up residence in a human host. The next week I called my brother to see how Nicole was doing. I didn't want to tell Nicole I was responsible for her breakup. Paul told me Nicole was doing great. Nicole's boyfriend wanted to get back together with her. Nicole didn't want to resume the relationship and started dating other young men. I felt much better about the clearing I had done and it looked like things had worked out for the best regarding Nicole.

Lurking Energy Vampires

You never know how things will turn out when you're working in the spirit realm. When Paul Miller, the healer, was changing the energy at Jesse's office to protect her from the energy drain she was experiencing, I never expected the melt down at her office brought on by Gwen, one of her good friends she worked with. The changes Paul made at Jesse's office looked bleak for Jesse that first month. But her good friend Gwen got fired for not showing up to work. Gwen, after getting fired, went to work for another company. After Gwen was gone from the office Jesse started feeling better. It looked to me that Gwen was the energy vampire in the office that was stealing a great deal of energy from Jesse and everyone that worked there.

Jesse was suffering side effects caused by an energy vampire: anxiety, having low energy and wondering why a friend would cause such havoc to herself and others. The great news is, in five months after the fall out at Jesse's office, Jesse was off anti-depressants and back to her high energy, over-achieving self. Another case of an energy vampire having no regard for the destructive drain of life force they caused another human being.

All the healing work I was doing with Paul Miller was paying off. I was learning to protect and clear myself effectively enough to stop DL from draining my energy most of the time. The visits I made to the Vibe machine twice a week for 20 minutes raised my energy. I noticed while I was sitting by the Vibe machine DL couldn't steal my life force. DL was unable to locate me, send beings after me, use the dark arts to find me or send psychic energy vampire cords to cause holes in my aura and steal my life force. The Vibe machine is a device that creates energy and light, giving me a powerful sanctuary (no DL zone) of light and energy where dark energies can't survive. My goal these past two years has been to raise the energy level of my aura. According to the energy vampire book if I can heal my aura to 100% DL would no longer be able to affect me in any manner. Along the way I have been learning how to help others who have been suffering devastation in their lives from energy vampires.

Skiing Winter of 2011

The snow fall totals in the mountains this winter were piling up. I had already been out skiing four times this winter to get in shape so I could ski with my friend Barbara. Having one snow storm after another, blanketing the ski slopes, added up to quite a few feet of snow which makes for great skiing. No ice, rocks, bushes or small pine trees to ski over that could possibly knock me down. Deep natural snow, not man-made snow, is fun to ski on. My skis were made to carve turns but the better the snow the easier my skis carve a turn.

Barbara and I skied a half day at Winter Park and I was able to keep up. It was only a half day but I could tell I was getting stronger and I was feeling no pain. When DL isn't stealing energy from me while I'm skiing the day after skiing I recover my energy in a day. If DL is stealing energy while I'm skiing, I'm in pain and it takes me a week to recover my energy from a half day of skiing. I actually remember why I've enjoyed skiing so much all of my life…because it's fun! But when DL crashes my party and decides I need some company while I'm skiing it is a big drag. Hence the name Dragon Lord.

February 14th of 2011 on Monday Paul Miller and I traded out another session. I always look forward to my sessions with Paul. Paul and I have become good friends over the past two years. There aren't many people you can talk shop with about the spiritual realm. It's informative to share how we're dealing with beings and what we have been learning about the spiritual realm.

For me I have a friend who totally gets what I have been going through and is supportive of my spiritual growth. I was excited to thank Paul for working with my daughter. Jesse is off anti-depressants, has no more anxiety and Gwen, her so-called friend the energy vampire, is out of her life for good. Paul Miller is the most powerful healer that I have worked with and since Paul has been working with me I have seen amazing results. I send thanks to the higher powers for guiding this loving, kind, humble man and healer into my life.

For my session today Paul was helping me clean my chakras. I was able to see the gold energy that my chakras produce. For the first time I can see the greenish color, I call it army green, surrounding the gold energy of my chakras caused from DL's energy vampire attacks. The greenish virus covering film that feeds like a parasite on the victim's aura, Paul helped remove from my chakras. After Paul cleared away the greenish film from my chakras I was able to see the gold color energy of my chakras. I tested with my pendulum and my vital energy, after 8 years from the day in January that I first worked with DL, was finally back to a healthy 100%. I felt great, the way I felt before Dragon Lord infected my life. The session with Paul was the best Valentine's gift ever. The gift of vital energy! It has taken Paul two years to repair the damage that DL had inflicted to my aura and my health because of her lust for others' energy. Dragon Lord, a shaman who professes to be a healer but in truth is only a societal parasite.

The 10th of March Barbara and I picked a sunny, amazing ski conditions day at Winter Park to ski. This is what I call the perfect ski day. Warm enough to wear sunglasses and a head band. The snow was fresh and soft, easy to carve a turn in. I could tell the difference in my skiing performance and energy. It was the first time in years that I wanted to stay and ski the entire day.

Life is good! I've waged the battle against the dark energies and

I've won my life back. What an amazing journey this has been for me…the higher powers guiding me to learn the extent of my psychic gifts and how to use them to help others break away from energy vampires. Divine guidance has helped me to meet other healers that serve the light that are true healers. May my book guide you to healers that serve the light. I wish blessings of love and light to all who read my book.

THE END

Colophon

Text set in
Minion Pro
Titles in Titania
Using Adobe Indesign
Printed USA

www.onespiritpress.com
onespiritpress@gmail.com

www.ingramcontent.com/pod-product-compliance
Lightning Source LLC
Chambersburg PA
CBHW070755100426
42742CB00012B/2136